Charlie and Shirley,

Thank you for being such
wonderful friends to our
family over the years

Dick Brogden Jr

30-7-09

PUBLISHED BY STEEPLE BOOKS
www.steeple.com

SteepleBooks is an evangelical Christian publisher dedicated to bringing God and people together. We believe God's vision for SteepleBooks is to enable Christian authors to publish biblical, meaningful, and inspirational materials. SteepleBooks provides editorial, production, marketing, sales, and distribution services for authors. *For a free catalog of resources from* SteepleBooks, *please contact us at* www.steeple.com or send an e-mail to info@steeple.com.

Loving Muslims
Copyright © 2009 by Dick Brogden

Except where otherwise indicated, Bible quotations are taken from New King James Version of the Bible. Copyright 1982 by Thomas Nelson, Inc. (Nashville, TN).

Edited by Jackie A. Chapman
Cover design by Andy Beachum

For more information about the author and his ministry, address all correspondence to dickbrogden@gmail.com.

Brogden, Dick
     Loving Muslims / by Dick Brogden.
          p.   cm.
     ISBN 978-0-9821240-2-4
     Summary: "Using biblical examples from a lifetime of ministry, Dick Brogden gives a message of hope for those who would answer the call of God to minister to Muslims."--Provided by publisher.

     1. Islam--Relations--Christianity. 2. Christianity and other religions--Islam. 3. Missions to Muslims. I. Title

Printed in the United States of America.

LOVING MUSLIMS

DICK BROGDEN

Loving Muslims

Forward

The Sudanese people are without peer. They are gracious, loving and hospitable. Jennifer and I sincerely believe that the Sudanese are the most wonderful of God's varied people. We love the Sudanese. We love Muslims.

After 16 years in the Muslim world, I feel it necessary to draw a distinction between Muslims and Islam. I have seen firsthand the result of practical Islam. While I love Muslims, I cannot say the same for Islam. While there is some similarity between the monotheistic faiths of Christianity and Islam, there are also crucial distinctions.

It is not politically correct in this day and age to say anything negative about Islam. While functional free speech allows any amount of ridicule directed towards the Bible, Christ or Christians, it frowns upon any negative assessment of Islam.

Regardless I respectfully say that I disagree with and personally reject Islam. In the same way that any human has the liberty to reject and disagree with Christ, I do so with Islam and insist upon my right to do so with civility and malice towards none. Any anger that might result from the content of this book will merely prove my point. In a world that champions free speech, there must be room for the voice that says, "Islam has been tried and found wanting."

Muslims, on the other hand, are a totally different story. And yes, you can differentiate between Muslims and Islam. Islam is a system of belief. Muslims are people. They are kind, humorous, giving, forgiving, loving and gracious. They are fathers, mothers, children, friends and colleagues. I love Muslims; they are my friends. It is my hope that you, too, will come to love Muslims.

Dick Brogden – Sudan, Africa

Loving Muslims

Dedication

This book is dedicated to friends and teammates who diligently and systematically give their lives to serve Muslims. Some of you are Sudanese and some of you are not. Some of you have shared in the work for a short time; some of you have endured far longer than I have. Together we have laughed, cried, prayed, brainstormed, worried, feared, stumbled and risen to press on. From all of you I have learned something; to all of you I owe a debt of gratitude. My deepest debt is owed to Maajid Benjamin. He is a chip off The Mighty Rock.

It is my hope that the events recorded below will challenge many new laborers to answer the call of the Harvest Master to join us in the field. There are many fields of labor; none perhaps so desperate as those in Islamic lands. As you read this book, may Jesus stir you to come help us. Come by your prayers. Come in your weakness. Come with your fears. Jesus is more than able to use stammering lips to work great victory.

My own journey to the Harvest has been progressive. I did not have a sensational call that led me to where I am now like my father did. My father as a young man after a camp meeting saw Jesus at the end of his bed when Jesus specifically told him that he would be a missionary in Africa. My calling is just as sure but radically different. As a young child I felt in my heart that God wanted me to serve Him in full-time ministry. There were no bells, whistles or lightning bolts, just a calm assurance. I stood gazing at the starry African sky spread over the great Rift Valley one night while in high school and I knew, without voices or telegrams, that God was defining the service He wanted of me as missionary. After a year in bible school during a convention that features speakers from the Islamic world, the same steady Holy Spirit impressed upon me that my missionary service was to concentrate on Islamic peoples.

And step-by-step God led me to this point. He never knocked me over the head with a rubber hammer but He guided me by these principles:

1) His heart is a missionary heart and it beats for the lost.
2) There are ridiculously few missionaries working amongst Muslims and incredible numbers of Muslims that die daily without Christ.
3) The Biblical understanding of the word "missionary" ("apostle") is one who goes where there is no gospel witness and establishes one.
4) My wife must share the calling with me and receive it independently from me.
5) Those to whom I am accountable will confirm my vision and call.

As you pray for the Muslim world and God's leading on your life, He will lead you as you learn to lean.

Contents

Loving Muslims
Introduction

This book is a collection of missionary letters: some of them light, others serious. They are arranged chronologically, written from Sudan, a country where Islam rules yet Jesus reigns. It is my prayer that the simple lessons contained in these pages will draw you closer to the Father heart of God. His Father heart resounds with passion for those who do not yet know Him. Sudan, as you will see, is a land of tremendous paradox combining tragedy and triumph, poverty and resource, cursing and blessing in a heart-rending mosaic.

Part One

GREETINGS FROM THE LAND OF...

E-mails from Sudan

LAND OF VISITORS

Resident on our porch are two baby pigeons. They get the walking part but they stand on the rail looking down like scared adolescents on the high dive. One morning when Jennifer woke up, one of them had entered the house and perched on her chest. We look forward to the day when they move on for they are not yet potty trained.

A slightly better behaved but less affectionate visitor arrived in the capital today. His name is Rafsanjani and he is the president of Iran. Sudan does not have many friends on the international stage and the few she does have are not the most favorable ones. Ironically the Iranian president is here to try and broker a peace between Sudan and one of her enemies. Have you ever pictured the current Iranian regime as a peacemaker?

A third visitor dropped in last night: Mr. Haboob. A haboob is a fierce sandstorm that blows in off the Sahara. Our bedroom is too hot to sleep in. So every night we drag our mattresses out to the balcony or the sitting room area where we can sometimes catch a faint breeze. Last night when the haboob dropped in, uninvited, we woke up covered in fine sand. This is the third time it has happened, and each time it does we sweep out piles of sand from the house.

We have heard about another visitor who is allegedly on his way to our city. No one is sure whether how much is truth or fiction. This is the rumor. Two weeks ago some army generals attempted a coup. The government suppressed the uprising and executed most of the officers. Rumor has it that some officers escaped and took over the port city in the East. They are said to have blown up the railroad and the pipeline link to the capital; some even say they are advancing on this city. If the above is true, some exciting times lie ahead. For now, life goes on as normal as we wait to see what is truth and what is rumor.

Visitation is an important part of Sudanese culture. Most visits occur in the evening from 7 to 10 o'clock. Everyone reclines on beds, usually on a balcony or porch, drinking tea. Sometimes a whole meal is offered. Sudanese are incredibly generous and will go to extremes to be of service to you. Even in these days of incredible financial difficulty, they receive visitors with great respect and careful attention. We long for the day when Sudanese will receive a special visit from "on high" and welcome that visitor with arms as open as is customary for mere mortals.

LAND OF NOTHING

Sudan is a country with few resources yet she struggles valiantly to make do. Here are some examples, ranging from the trivial to the serious.

Books: A friend enrolled in the same Arabic course we did. The teacher told him he needed certain textbooks and that he should bring them to the next class. Our friend looked all over town but could not find any of the books. Upon returning to class the following day and telling his teacher of his fruitless search, the teacher replied, "Oh, you can only get those books in England."

Roads: North of our capital city there are precious few paved roads. You can take buses that follow tracks through the sand for hundreds of miles to various destinations. One bus set off through the desert for Libya and weeks later ended up in Chad. Another bus carrying a Christian pastor and 30 others got lost. All aboard perished due to insufficient water supplies.

Zoo food: Zoo food? A family with small children went to visit the sparsely populated city zoo and found only a few animals and snakes. The zookeepers, wanting to impress the foreigners, brought out a cute, young, alive puppy and fed it to the snake. The parents had to hustle their crying children away.

Air travel: Two months ago a passenger plane from a southern city was approaching the capital and arrived at the exact same time as a haboob did. The pilot was instructed to fly to another city since he could not locate the airport due to swirling sand. Though he had ample fuel to reach the suggested city, he refused and circled the city for two hours before running out of fuel and crashing, killing all 60 passengers on board.

Sudan is quite a place. I saw a dog in the dirty streets with a broken back that had taught itself to walk on two feet. The dog swung its useless legs out in front and walked on its two front feet, balancing amazingly well.

Living in Africa can be a gut-wrenching experience. As a missionary kid I thought that I had grown accustomed to staring in the face of abject poverty. Not that I was callous. I was aware of suffering and moved by it but not overwhelmed. But that perception of myself was severely tested today. I have never seen poverty and suffering to the extent of that here in Sudan. With the prolonged civil war, there has been a mass relocation of displaced people to this Muslim city in the north. Jobs do not existent and hunger is abundant; the economy is crippled and inflation is servant to none.

Every day when I take out my garbage, there is a man who waits patiently in order to dig through it, looking for scraps of food. He is not just another starving statistic. His name is William, he is well educated and he has three sons at home. I know because I talk with him.

Today William had competition. As I walked toward the dumpster that sits in a large open field, I noticed there were three other men picking through the heaped up garbage. A fourth man, carrying a bundle of rags some distance away, picked up his pace as he saw me approach. "Peace upon you," I said as I threw my trash on the heap. "And upon you be peace," rejoined one of the men as the others scrambled for my pitiful garbage. They fought over those two pathetic plastic bags. In the ensuing struggle the bags burst and the contents were scattered.

I have now given out more benevolence than ever in my life. It has never been demanded and is usually humbly received. It is never enough. It does not calm the churning of my stomach nor does it erase the pitiful pictures that crowd my thoughts whenever I close my eyes. Africa continually amazes me. Somehow, some way, the people and creatures of this forsaken land struggle to survive. Somehow they persevere, plodding on through weary days.

The irony is that Sudanese are largely ignorant of their greatest lack: Jesus. Sudan is caught in the jaws of a problem that encompasses all economic levels. They have a desperate need to be lifted from the poverty of a deceptive religion and a hollow spiritual existence into the arms of a personal Savior. There are hundreds of thousands of square miles, millions of people, but scarcely any followers of the Crucified. Is there any hope?

Lest I leave you depressed, there are whispers and reports of the divine, the miraculous, and stories of whole people groups coming to Christ. Allow me to leave these stirrings of hope for another day and close by challenging you in three areas:

1) Let us not forget how blessed we are in the West.
2) Let us not forget our responsibility to the oppressed, physically and especially spiritually.
3) Let us bombard heaven for the sake of the lost.

LAND OF INFLUENCE

"How did such an evil person attain such a position of influence?" I asked as I sat in Ahmed's courtyard enjoying a cool drink made from the hibiscus flower.

A refreshing breeze was blowing in from the south. The trees bent gracefully in the wind, a pigeon cooed and an ewe let out a maternal bleat. The river in stately splendor continued its eternal journey 100 meters away.

Ahmed sat back in his chair with a thoughtful look in his eyes and shifted the position of the turban on his head. The turban moved as one piece, though it was wound several times. He remained quiet as I chewed on the palm dates that had been set before us. Ahmed is a university professor with excellent English so his long pause reflected his deep thought, not his lack of understanding. We had been talking for over an hour and a half. Our conversation had ranged from the serious to the silly.

"I think," Ahmed finally said, "that to do evil is easy and to do good almost impossible. Many people rise to positions of power through underhanded means. There are few good men in the world and even fewer in places of authority."

Our conversation moved to the depravity of man in a fallen

world. I told him that the Bible says, "There is no one that is good, not even one."

A cloud of despair seemed to settle down on Ahmed. I felt prompted by the Holy Spirit to press on. For the next few minutes, I briefly talked about the fall of man and how the curse of sin entered the world through the first Adam. I then quoted an excerpt from one of my favorite Christmas hymns "Joy to the World," "He comes to make his blessings known, far as the curse is found!" and said, "Ahmed, Jesus, the second Adam, is the one, the only one, through whom freedom from the curse comes."

Ahmed got up to look for his Koran but couldn't find it. He was visibly moved and he seemed at a loss as far as what to do or what to say.

Later when it was time to go, I stood and thanked Ahmed for the time and all I had learned. "I, too, have learned many things today," he said softly.

Please pray for Ahmed and the countless thousands he represents. He has not yet come to Christ but is perhaps much closer than yesterday. Please pray we will know what to say and when. Pray the Lord will continue to bring us in contact with those whom he has been calling. Pray that this mountain of Arabic language learning will be climbed, one step at a time.

LAND OF THE TEMPORARY

This week it is hot in Sudan. The nationals tell us it will cool down soon but it is still over 100 degrees. I asked a friend how many gallons of sweat you would lose in a year. He replied, "It depends on how overweight you are."

I had been bragging about how good the security is here compared to other places. Today our bubble burst and brought us to reality. I was in my bedroom working on the computer, waiting for Jennifer to return from a visit. Hearing the door open, I assumed she was home. Unfortunately, an uninvited visitor had helped himself to our portable tape recorder. I rushed from the apartment down four flights of stairs but the intruder had fled. Though we felt violated, this event pales in the light of eternity.

I went through the formality of making a police report in case, by slim chance, the tape recorder might be recovered. The process was a bit humorous. The police station, a run-down little place, is understaffed and overly busy. We made our way to the main desk and waited for someone to assist us. I noticed the room was sparsely furnished with only one beat-up file cabinet with doors so warped and rusted that an officer had to pry them open with a crowbar.

Another officer listened to our story and began to fill out a report. The process took a long time, as visitors pushed in around us yelling out their complaints or greetings, whichever. The officer laboriously completed our report in triplicate, without the use of carbon paper, pausing every few minutes to shake the hand of a long-lost aunt or listen to someone else's sad tale.

Only a barred door separated the adjacent holding cells containing the recently arrested. The unlucky incarcerated ones gathered at the door and listened eagerly to our story, shouting advice as to whom the thief was and where we could find him. We finally were sent to another office accompanied by a different officer. He repeated the same questions and added some of his own astute ones like, "Was the tape recorder plugged in when it was stolen?" I wasn't sure how that would help them find it but then again I did not take a private investigating class in Bible college. Three forms and endless questions later our report was completed. Will it help? Maybe, but most likely not.

In a country like Sudan, this incident makes us thankful for what we have. This week a Christian lady was sentenced to death by stoning because she allegedly committed adultery. Her partner, a Muslim, merely swore on the Koran that he was innocent and was promptly released. The lady is currently pregnant. What does a tape recorder matter to her? May Jesus continually remind us of the eternal souls he came to redeem. All this wood, hay and stubble is nice, but temporary.

LAND OF LANGUAGE
Perhaps some of you know that Sudan has over 200 languages.

Our first task is to learn the trade language, Arabic. The colloquial Arabic spoken on the street, however, is very different than the classical language used on the radio or on the printed page. We are in effect learning two languages. I am writing to tell you a little bit about that effort. And yes, the use of the word "effort" is intentional.

The university here supplies our visas in Sudan but its language program is disorganized and inadequate. Classes were supposed to begin the first week of August but two months later we are still waiting. Our real language learning takes place at an "unofficial" language institute run by Catholics. We have classes four hours a day, five days a week, with four hours a day of study, practice and homework.

Our class membership is diverse consisting of two Eritreans, three Koreans, one Italian, two Indians, one Sudanese and one from Myanmar (formerly Burma). I speak Swahili to communicate with the Sudanese student, the Eritreans speak Italian to the Italian, and the man from Myanmar speaks Hindi to the Indians. In general a lot of head shaking, hand wagging and "what did you say?" queries dominate the conversations.

I (Dick) was voted class representative to the director of the school. Some of my more important duties are cleaning the blackboard and dusting with a dust cloth. With all the different dialects of broken English floating around, Jennifer and I were amused one day when a professor declared, "I can understand everyone here but those two Americans!"

A member of our class is lagging behind a bit in his studies and I was impatient with him until he told me that Arabic is his 11th language!

The other day we were working on translation. Much to the delight of the rest of our class, one of the Koreans enunciated, "My Arabic professor is a donkey!" The professor was not very amused.

So we continue on with heads full of the endless little rules and exceptions of Arabic grammar. A Swedish lady who has been in Sudan for several years puts it this way (this is my paraphrase),

"In the West we are consumed with activity and doing. Not so the Arabs. To them relationship and conversation are the ideals. Consequently their language has evolved, becoming more precise and detailed. The highest honor goes to those who are most articulate."

That is why we are studying. We want to give them Jesus but we must know their language and their culture to accurately present the good news. Thank you for your prayers for us, your representatives in this wonderful land.

LAND OF PUBLIC TRANSPORT

Or the lack of it as the case might soon be. The United Nations is considering leveling an embargo against Sudan Airlines next month. Speculation abounds as to whether that will happen and if it does, what the effect will be. Generally, people think that Sudan Airlines will fold. International flights are the main source of revenue and domestic flights will be shut down as well. Some think this will affect all the other airlines, meaning that it would be impossible to get in or out of Sudan, at least by air. Needless to say we are hoping that is not the case. Some Filipino friends are planning a route of "departure" by land across the desert to Libya and from there to Egypt.

Closer to home, we have been enjoying the buses and other forms of public service available in the city. We used to take taxis but they were too expensive at the whopping rate of $3 per hour. We usually take the bus for 10 cents a trip. The buses are nice; sometimes you can even find a seat. When your stop approaches, you loudly snap your fingers or hiss between your teeth and the driver pulls over to let you off. Sometimes when they pick you up, they don't come to a complete stop. You have to run along side and swing yourself in. The first time I tried, I smashed my face into the folding door, much to the amusement of the passengers.

The bus drivers compete among themselves as to who can have the gaudiest dashboard. They display numerous kinds of decoration: stuffed peacocks, silk flowers and Easter egg ensembles, IV bags hanging from the rear view mirror, huge potted plants, a lunch box and assorted carpeting on the dashboard, walls and rear view mirror complete with flashing red lights that say "LOVE" whenever the driver steps on the brakes.

Another form of transport called a cage costs an economical 7 cents a ride. This three-ton truck is lined with benches along the length of the bed and is covered with a tin roof with metal bars for sides. The first people who get in sit down and others crowd around. Those fortunate to have a seat also have the polite custom of holding the briefcase, purse or luggage of the one standing. The first time this happened to Jennifer, she wasn't sure what was happening and a tug-of-war ensued as she tried to pull her purse out of the helping hands of her fellow traveler. And if the cage is full, you can always hang on the back. A few weeks ago I was hanging on for dear life...with a stranger hanging on to me.

The final form of transport is a small minivan converted into something like a sardine can. Not many foreigners use this so we are usually treated with respect, looked at curiously and always ripped off. We do enjoy the contact with the friendly Sudanese.

LAND OF PROGRESS

We continue to study Arabic, daunted by how far we have to go and encouraged by how far we have come. We continue to make friends with Algerian diplomats, Sudanese neighbors, language teachers, other teammates and people from various walks of life.

One friend is Ibrahim. Today as our Arabic lessons came to a close, we decided to visit him. Two days earlier when I visited him, he was deathly ill. But today Ibrahim looked even worse than before. His flesh seemed to have shrunk to a thin layer of skin stretched over bone. He tried to rise to greet us but couldn't.

We sat down in the breezeway common to traditional Sudanese houses. The afternoon sun cast its relentless gaze on the sun-baked land. Pigeons fluttered by our heads and ants crawled over our feet. Ibrahim seemed to fade in and out of consciousness. He then became restless. "I am so anxious," he told me. "I have tried every bed in this house! I need a change."

"Would you like me to read to you?" I asked.

"Yes!" Ibrahim said. "Yes!" said his daughter, wiping the tears of worry from her eyes with her tobe, a seamless piece of material Sudanese women wrap around themselves from head to toe.

"Would you mind if I read from the Bible?" I asked.

Ibrahim nodded his assent silently. I took a deep breath and sent up a quick prayer. Opening to Peter, I read about the prayer of faith healing the sick. The door of the compound flew open with a bang, heralding the arrival of a visitor. I quickly hid the Bible. Ibrahim was unfazed. He waved weakly with his hand and said huskily, "Keep reading please."

I then read the account of the sick man being lowered through the roof and other stories about Jesus healing people. When I came to the story of the healing of the paralytic, Ibrahim's eyes lit up and he turned to his daughter, saying in Arabic, "The Messiah, people even climbed through the roof to get to him!"

As I began to read again, I was interrupted by Ibrahim's daughter, "Dick, you can pray for him if you want." I put down the Bible slowly, trying to conceal my surprise. I did not want to offend him, so I asked, "May I pray for you?" He nodded.

"May I lay my hands on you?" Another nod. With grateful hearts and a simple prayer we asked Jesus, who has healed so many in days gone by, to heal again. Please pray the healing will spread to his soul as well.

Yes, Sudan is a land of progress, a land where God is moving. He does not always move in our timetables but he is faithfully reaching out to the Sudanese that he desperately loves. Can we even bear to think of the countless Ibrahims who need to hear the truth? Let us, out of love and not out of guilt, rededicate ourselves to our Father's business.

LAND OF WAITING

After what seems like an interminable wait, winter has finally come. Yes, it is true. We often have a slight breeze and the temperature plummeted all the way down to the low 90s. At night, we even cover up with a sheet. We love it. It is amazing how cool the 90s are when you have been sweltering at 130 degrees.

Patience is now needed for any form of transport. A few days ago the government put an advertisement in the paper saying, "DO NOT WORRY, WE HAVE PLENTY OF PETROL!" That means, of course, that there is none. So everyone rushes frantically to the gas stations. Cars line up three and four deep and stretch for several kilometers from every gas station. A friend of ours waited in line for six hours. When he finally got to the front, he could only get two gallons at over $4 per gallon. We continue to use public transport but it is getting more crowded every day.

Time is also looked at differently. Some Swedish friends just returned to Sweden after a year in Sudan. They had become good friends with a Sudanese family. As the time of their departure approached, the family wanted to give our friends a special gift by which to remember them. They gave them an unusual family picture – unusual because it was over 12 years old. The parents were barely recognizable – let alone the children!

This country is also unusual because entry visas are only slightly more difficult to get than exit visas. One relief worker waited for eight months after he finished his work, denied permission to leave. Others have found ways to expedite the system, sometimes unwittingly. In a meeting that was becoming increasingly frustrating, a foreign worker picked up a book and slammed it on the table. "We are getting nowhere!" he exclaimed.

The room went deathly quiet. He had without realizing it chosen to slam down the Koran. In four hours he was sky-bound on the first plane out of here. Another relief worker, so agitated by the endless delay, dropped his drawers and mooned the government official. His exit visa was immediately granted. This method is not recommended by most...

We continue to wait on Arabic. Or more precisely Arabic continues to wait for us. Both our teachers and our friends show mercy by not punishing us for slaughtering their language. We keep plodding.

LAND OF PUBLIC ORDER

A few days ago, new regulations were published in the newspaper under the heading "Public Order Act." Let me quote a few:

- Men and women should sit separately with dividing curtains at parties, in clubs or on farms, etc.
- Women should not sit beside the driver.
- Women should be accompanied at night shopping with a legal chaperone like a father, son, husband or brother.
- Women's sports should be under lock and key, away from men's eyes.
- Service places and shops near girls' schools should not have tinted glass or curtains. The door should be open and the premises brightly lit.

The list goes on, mostly to the disadvantage of women. We were favorably impressed when we first arrived at the freedom women enjoyed, especially in comparison to places like Iran and Afghanistan. But it seems that now is changing. A friend of ours saw a man and a woman arrested at a bus stop this week, simply for talking to each other. How earnestly these rules will be implemented no one is sure now.

I was a little distracted with my own public order problem this week. Have you ever gone shopping in a foreign country for something for which you did not know the word? Have you ever had to draw the object, or in a more desperate case pantomime it? An object like a toilet seat?

Alas, it is true. Our toilet seat was broken and I bravely set out to attempt to buy a new one. Our Arabic vocabulary is increasing but we have not seen a chapter on toilets yet. Not a problem, I thought. I will simply sketch it out. I went into a store and after the customary greetings, asked for a pen and paper. After a Picasso-like attempt, the storekeeper cocked an eyebrow at me and said quizzically, "You want a stereo?"

I could see I was in trouble. I remembered too late that the majority of Sudanese do not even use a western-style toilet. I was forced to my last recourse – pantomime.

Throughout the next hour, to the delight of the Sudanese shopkeepers, I was forced to act out a trip to the bathroom several times. It was often embarrassing and always humbling. This is just one more practical thing they never teach you in Bible school: How to say "toilet seat" in Arabic!

LAND OF IRONY

We had an interesting Thanksgiving last week. We invited 12 Muslims to celebrate with us. Jennifer worked hard and with our neighbor's help, she cooked a huge feast. Turkey, chicken, stuffing, potatoes, veggies and homemade pies filled the menu. We were surprised to find a turkey buried in the freezer of a grocery store. It had been there so long that boiling water and chipping at the ice could not get it out. They had to unplug the freezer and let it thaw before we could buy it.

Before the meal I explained the origin of Thanksgiving and related how the Pilgrim Fathers took time, after the first harvest, to thank Almighty God. I mentioned how thankful we were for our home country and the freedom we enjoyed there but that religious freedom does not guarantee a relationship with God.

After a short prayer, we ate the wonderful meal, relaxed a bit and enjoyed the pies. An intense discussion then began. For over three hours, I was peppered with questions: some of them sincere while probing, others attacking, intending to trip me up.

Jennifer retired to the bedroom and began to pray. During those hours I was able to give a simple, yet clear, gospel witness, reading many Scriptures. At times the group was loud and cynical; at other times subdued and wondering. We were able to scatter seed, though we don't know the condition of the soil.

The irony in the situation is that the 12 Muslims were all Americans. These young men between the ages of 18 and 26 had come to Sudan to study Arabic and Islam. Far from home, they were missing pizza and McDonalds. Islam was different than they had imagined. Their hearts had been deceived and hardened by the enemy of their souls. How wonderful and strange it would be if they came halfway around the world in a vain cause only to discover the Lover of their souls!

We came halfway around the world to reach the Sudanese, which by his grace we will. Isn't it remarkable that God has sent lost Americans to our door? I can't help but think of the many Muslims now living in the States – your friends, your neighbors, your co-workers, perhaps even your relatives. God has sent them to you. I plead with you to give them the Light. Don't hide it under a bushel, behind the wall of busyness or beneath the blanket of fear.

In the final analysis, we don't have ultimate control over those with whom we come in contact. That is arranged by the Master Planner. We don't have control over who will yield to the soft calling of the Holy Spirit. We can't force anyone or even intellectually persuade him or her to come to faith. By its definition, faith must be personal, simple and optional. What a miracle it is that ANYONE is saved! But they are, both here and there. Let us ask the Father for more of his Spirit that we might better witness of his Son.

LAND OF PATIENCE

The opportunity to learn patience is always available! It remains to be seen (irony intended) whether I am acquiring that noble virtue. Thursday morning we leave for a missions conference in Ethiopia. I have run around like crazy (i.e. run to an office and sat like crazy), trying to get the paperwork in order. Here is a brief synopsis of African red tape.

Relations between Sudan and Ethiopia have deteriorated to the point where it isn't possible to fly directly from Sudan to Ethiopia. This means we have to get a visa via Kenya or Egypt. We also needed a visa to leave Sudan, which meant getting a letter from our employer.

This is where my odyssey began Monday morning. I approached the director of the Arabic institute and after the usual 15-minute chitchat, I got around to my reason for being there. After I made my request for a letter he said, "Well, maybe come back Thursday or maybe Saturday. I might be here one of those days and I might write it."

Hardly a ringing endorsement!

But I went back Thursday and surprise! He was there and wrote the letter on a piece of scratch paper. Now if only he could find a typist to type it. The typist was on an eternal break. When she finally showed up, she took 45 minutes to type one paragraph. The director finally shuffled back in with the letter. He was about to sign it when he realized there was a small error. Back to the typist, it must go. But you guessed it. The typist had gone back to her break. After what seemed like forever, she was found and did her 45-minute hunt-and-peck job all over again.

From there the letter had to go with our passports to the Department of Internal Affairs (usually the most difficult part of the process), but a Sudanese friend has a friend in the office and our visas were hustled through in a stunning three days. From there, I went to the Kenyan embassy where I got our visas in a lightning-quick three hours. From there, I went to the Ethiopian embassy where I ran smack dab into a wall.

The Ethiopian embassy requires a letter from your international organization, paid airline tickets, international health cards and a letter from your embassy. I was able to furnish all of these except the letter from the embassy. Our embassy staff has left Sudan and an official flies from Cairo every three weeks for a few days. A skeletal Sudanese crew is available but doesn't have authority to issue a letter. So back and forth I went. Three hours in the American embassy, calling the administrative officer in Kenya. His answer, "Well, if it were an emergency, I would help you." Back at the Ethiopian embassy, for four hours I tried to explain that a letter wasn't possible. They sent me back to the American embassy and from there back to the Ethiopian, and on it went. I read every magazine in both waiting rooms, learned all the security guards by their first names and made lifelong friends of six different taxi drivers.

You get the picture. This went on for a week to no avail. Yesterday I went for one final time to the Ethiopian embassy and asked for the 100th time to see the counselor. "He is not in," smiled the receptionist, as I watched the man in question walk into his office.

"Can I make an appointment?" I asked.

"You have to call to do that." He smiled.

"Who do I call?" I asked.

"You have to call me." He smiled.

I must have looked like I was going to cry or maybe it was the banging of my head against the window of his booth, for he relented and gave me an appointment.

Jennifer and I prayed about it and the next day I had to wait a mere 30 minutes before the smiling attendant called out, "JENNIFER!" For the last week and a half, he had been calling me Jennifer but today I did not mind.

After a half-hour meeting with the counselor, I was sent back to the waiting room where I re-read some old papers. "Jennifer," my buddy called again. I bounded up to his window and paid the seven dollars per passport. Once more I returned to the old newspapers. An hour later I had the visas in hand. Whew!

LAND OF PROTECTION

We arrived home safely from Ethiopia and Kenya. After the barren desert of Sudan, these countries felt like heaven. We had a great time of refreshment and renewal. One day as I was driving through Eldoret, a Kenyan town where we used to live, I noticed a nice-looking man with a soccer shirt. "Hey," I thought, "that looks like my favorite college soccer shirt." I did a double take. It WAS my old soccer shirt (same number and everything), which had been stolen from our house two years ago. May he wear it with pride!

Flying back into Sudan's capital at night, I was struck with the immensity of the city. Living here, you think the city is small since it has a "laidback" feel. Flying in at night and seeing the lights stretch out in all directions reminds you that seven million people live within a few square kilometers. Nearly all seven million need the light of the Morning Star.

As we settle in again, we feel a tangible heavy oppression. We find ourselves arguing about senseless things, frustrated over minute details and discouraged at minor obstacles. Sometimes I take a mental time-out to realize anew we really are in a spiritual struggle. It is then that I think, "I hope someone is praying for us!" Thank you for lifting us up.

Let me share two simple Sudanese experiences. Our language school is directly across the street from the city hospital. Before Christmas break, we noticed the water had begun to taste funny and had a musty smell. The hospital noticed it and decided to investigate the water tank. They found a decaying human body floating in it. The poor man had been viciously murdered and dumped in the water supply.

Speaking of disposing of evidence, sometime ago we received a packet of mail via courier that contained the word "missionary" and other sensitive statements that could compromise our security. We put the pile in the sink to burn it. Soon our whole house was filled with smoke and it began to stream out of the windows. I tried to douse the flames but succeeded only in wetting the ashes, making them stick to everything.

Being high-tech experts, we have devised an alternate solution. After reading the letters, we rip out the sensitive sections, stuff them in our mouths and chew them until they are illegible. We learned this trick from a local bus driver. When a passenger gave him his ticket, the driver calmly stuffed it in his mouth and chewed it up. This advanced technique not only ensures our privacy, it cuts down on our grocery bills! So if your water smells or if you are wondering how to keep private letters private, now you know what to do. And you thought nothing good could come out of "Sudanazareth."

LAND THAT IS WEARY

"Beneath the cross of Jesus I fain would take my stand,
The shadow of a mighty rock within our weary land,
A home within the wilderness, a rest upon the way,

PART ONE

From the burning of the noontide heat, and the burden of the day."
— "Beneath the Cross of Jesus" by Elizabeth Clephane (emphasis added)

That has been our testimony. No other place do we long to be but beneath the Cross. No other refuge do we seek but in the shadow of the mighty rock. He truly is our home and our rest. There is a temptation in our line of work to pump out success stories and good reports, being conscious of our accountability to you, the ones who hold us up. We would be remiss, however, as would you, if we gained the world and lost our soul. Jesus loves us too much for that.

In the last few weeks, Jennifer and I have felt the gentle tug of the Holy Spirit. He has been calling us to be with him, to know him better, to press in further. He has reminded us that what we do is secondary to what we are. He is teaching us that as we are with him, we will become like him. When we are like him, we will draw others. Being flesh, we are slow learners and often look to people, success or ourselves for encouragement, peace and fulfillment. Again and again that search proves futile and we are brought back to the truth, "All that thrills my soul is Jesus."

The third verse of the above hymn states:

*"I take, O cross, thy shadow For my abiding place,
I ask no other sunshine than The sunshine of His face;
Content to let the world go by, To know no gain or loss,
My sinful self my only shame, My glory all the cross."*

Paradoxically, as we "let the world go by" and abide in him, he brings the world to us. We are amazed at how easy ministry is when we rest on him and what a struggle ensues when we try to push through on our own. In recent days, there have been unusual developments that I can't share now except to say he has clearly shown it is HIS work and HE IS PREVAILING against the gates of hell. Please pray with us.

January 10 marked the beginning of Ramadan, the month when all devout Muslims fast from sunup to sundown. They take no food and no drink for the whole day. In general, there is greater commitment to religious things – attendance at the mosque goes up, activity in the day goes down. There seems to be more openness but there are more attacks, revealing again that it is not flesh and blood but powers and principalities that we are up against.

No one is allowed to sell prepared food during the day. Office hours are shortened. A lethargic spirit descends on all. As the sun sets, the normally crowded streets resemble a ghost town. Everyone rushes home to break the day's fast. Woe to you if you happen to be driving just before the prayer call announces the sun has set. Cars speed by furiously. Everyone is anxious to get home and join the party. Ironically, more food is consumed during Ramadan than any other month. There are also more deaths at this time.

> "Upon that cross of Jesus, Mine eye at times can see
> The very dying form of One, Who suffered there for me
> And from my stricken heart with tears, Two wonders I confess
> The wonders of redeeming love, And my unworthiness"

We are rediscovering the wonder of dwelling beneath the cross. It is a journey and we often take wrong turns but we press on. We invite you to travel with us, to gaze again long and hard at our wonderful Savior rather than at your work, responsibilities or problems. You will find in running to Jesus and lingering beneath his cross, your work and vision is not discarded but prioritized, fulfilled and completed. Try it and be blessed.

LAND OF BLESSING

I am increasingly learning that "difficulty" and "difficult times" are relative terms. We attended a conference in Addis and in Nairobi during our recent trip. Christmas Eve found us in Kenya staying with long-time family friends and we went caroling in the hospitals with them.

I do not think anyone has ever volunteered to lay sick in

a dark, dirty hospital during days of warmth and celebration. The unfortunate in this hospital were no exception. Gloom had descended on all the poorly equipped wards. We saw a small child sitting on her mother's bed, a solitary spectator to the ravages of AIDS. Another bandaged child had lost her mother to a traffic accident. She was too young to know from where she had come or the name of her father, so she cowered alone in a strange, smelly world. Some patients shared beds, lying head to foot; others found space on the unforgiving cement floor. The wife of a patient stood on her husband's bed, and bending at the waist with knees locked straight, pulled his inert body up to a more comfortable position. Nearby a corpse gazed up lifeless, not yet removed to his final resting place.

The Land of Blessing? As we walked through the halls we sang Christmas carols, passed out fruit and prayed with each patient. As we sang "Joy to the World," the second verse reminded us, "He comes to make his blessings known, far as the curse is found!" The curse extends to all those who lie miserably in an African hospital on Christmas Eve, to those imprisoned by the unrelenting chains of sin, to selfish you and me. Yet to the extent of that curse and beyond, the mercy of Christ is found.

The Land of Blessing? Yes. In every land, to every suffering heart, to every trembling soul, the mercy of God is poured out. "Mercy there was great and grace WAS FREE." I looked out a window on my right and saw a Muslim in his white robe and skullcap, prostrate on the ground with his nose pressed to the ground in ritual prayer. Even to him? The blessing of God? Let it be.

I have been reminded we indeed are blessed beyond measure. How trivial some of my petty prayers must seem to the Father when compared to the needs of some of his children. Though my needs may be petty, he is gracious enough to hear them. I am also reminded that blessing goes far beyond health, wealth and security. To lead a dying soul to the Life Giver, to see the flicker of hope in empty eyes, to be rewarded with the shy smile of a bandaged infant is to be reminded that Jesus came and comes to make his blessings known.

LAND OF DELAY

Our visa here in Sudan is a student visa and our university classes were due to begin in August 1996. Let me quote from a letter Jennifer wrote to a friend to bring you up to date:

"The university class is meant to open on Monday. We have tried to register three times this week (after five months). The first day we went into the 10 x 12 foot office with two desks, five chairs and three "secretaries." They gave us two of the chairs to sit in while the "head" lady tried to help everyone at the same time. She discovered we had come to register so she began looking for a pen. Dick had already lent one to her earlier to sign her name to some man's form. Another girl dug into her purse and found one for her. Now she needed a piece of paper, preferably blank. She dug around, went through the file box on her desk and came up with something. Now she was ready for our names.

"Dick told her that we had been told that she had a list of all the students' names who had enrolled in that class. With that, she began looking in the bottom drawer of her desk and started shuffling through reams of loose papers. She went from drawer to drawer looking for this list without success. She did find other papers she must have needed though because she plopped a few forms on the desk and kept going.

"When she'd been through all its drawers and the box on the desk again, she apologized and said that it must have been misplaced. They didn't have such a paper. So now she wanted to write our names again but she had lost her original blank piece. After finding it in a drawer, the conversation went like this: 'OK, your names.' 'Dick Brogden, Jennifer Brogden.' 'Yes.' 'Do we pay you?' 'Yes.' 'Can we pay now?' 'No, I don't have any registration forms. Come back tomorrow or the next day, probably the day after tomorrow, and I will have them...'"

The next day, none. Four days later, not yet. The university is going broke; any guess as to why? Is there any chance that she can find the paper that she wrote our names on again?

Well, that was last week! Today I (Dick) went back again. Lo and behold, they had registration forms. The secretary smiled shyly and said, "Today we have the forms but not the receipt book. Please try another day." And so the deadlines pass. "Maybe next week" is the constant refrain.

It looked pretty certain we would begin this month but the war has flared up in the East. The rebels captured a few government towns and the powers that be are a little worried. In a speech on the radio last night, a general blamed the Ethiopians, Americans, British and Jews. Quite a conspiracy!

A few days ago, the President said he could enlist a million Sudanese to repel the invaders. All government universities were closed to enable students to enlist. By this afternoon a vast throng of 20 has done so.

We would be concerned about our Arabic studies but in the interim we have continued our private lessons five days a week and are swamped with grammar and vocabulary. If we look at how far we have come, we are encouraged. But if we look at how far we have to go...well, let's not talk about that!

LAND OF FASTING

We are now well into Ramadan, the Islamic month of fasting, a month when good deeds have extra merit, when a religious spirit pervades, when commitments are renewed and divine guidance is sought.

There are aspects of Ramadan that are festive and appealing. Since everyone is involved (at least outwardly), there is a common understanding and empathy. The fast is broken after sunset at a time announced by the imam from the tower of the mosque. Every evening below our window a large picnic blanket is spread and neighbors bring out their food for an impromptu potluck. Drinks, meats, fruit and sweets are freely shared and any passerby is invited to join in.

I do not know if I will do it every year but this year I am participating in the fast. I want to understand what it is like, the demands on body and soul. I want to express solidarity with my friends and neighbors. It also affords ample time for remembering them to the Father.

Last night we were invited to a friend's house to share in the daily breaking of the fast. Omar lives in a poor section of the city and his neatly kept house is made of old, crumbly bricks. The kitchen is symbolic of the clash of tradition and technology seen across Africa: a tiny unlit room with a sloping mud floor, complete with a modern gas stove and an electric blender.

As Jennifer helped the ladies prepare the meal, Omar and I took a stroll down to the nearby Nile. For the outing, he fitted me with a set of baggy white pirate pants (surwal), flowing white robe (jelaba) and white skullcap (tagia).

We walked through an irrigated field on the way to the river. A man in his 60s stood leaning on his hoe, with one foot resting on the inside of his other leg and his turban billowing in the breeze. He made a striking picture silhouetted against the setting sun. On the shores of the river there are numerous brick works. During the river's annual flood, a thick layer of silt washes down from the Ethiopian highlands, and when mixed with dried animal dung, it makes excellent bricks. These bricks are the main building material in Sudan and they create a brown city that blends in with the surrounding desert. As far as I could see in both directions, teams of men were mixing mud, shaping bricks, setting them out to dry, and building huge kilns in which to fire them. I felt as if I was looking at the supply site for Babel.

Bricks are made in a simple basin of mud, two at a time, in a crude wooden form. One man slops the mud into the forms while another hauls them off and places them in rows to dry. Others continually replenish the pile of mud.

To Omar's dismay I asked if I could try to make some bricks. The workmen cheerfully agreed and Omar hovered behind me, trying desperately to keep the sleeves of my white robe from splashing in the mud. Both the brick making and the preservation of the robe were a partial success.

We arrived back at the house just before the call to prayer and enjoyed a tasty traditional meal. The Sudanese will eat long into the night and even rise before daybreak for a light breakfast, before going through another day without food. One more day without. One more friend without. One more land without. It is tragic that all of their devotion, all of their effort and all of their sincerity are without meaning, for they are without the Meaningful One. By God's grace, it will not always be so. One day, at the great marriage breakfast of the Lamb, we trust this land will be well represented. Thank you for trusting with us.

LAND OF TRANSIENCE

This is a land where the only constant is change – a steady unraveling that is resignedly accepted, like the turban of the man in front of me on the bus. The persistent wind slowly unwound the carefully wrapped cloth until his bare head was exposed.

This morning Jennifer was feeling under the weather, so I set off to school by myself. Between our house and the bus stop, several refugee families from the South had erected homes from scattered bricks, mud and sticks. The humble shacks lean up against the immense homes of wealthy neighbors. As I passed by, I was greeted lustily with warm smiles and expressive waves. None of us could know that salutation was in effect a goodbye.

In the early afternoon, when I stepped off my bus, the area was in shambles. During the day a government official had come to pay a visit. He asked if they were Christian people. When they answered yes, their homes were destroyed. I gazed in despair at the mounds of rubble and broken furniture ruined by falling walls. The family members who were unfortunate enough to be home when the visit was paid were all arrested and imprisoned. They included grandmothers, children and a mother with a two-week-old baby.

Relatives now sifted through the rubble, stoically beginning to rebuild. My friend Peter, a cripple in a wheelchair, greeted me with a smile and a shrug. He had managed to salvage an old iron bed from the wreckage and had set it up between some piles of bricks. "I have nowhere to go," he said. "I might as well sleep here."

I moved on along the row of bulldozed houses. I was stunned to be greeted with smiles and warmth. The husband of the lady with the two-week-old baby was scooping debris out of his one-room abode. The walls were now razed to the ground. "I don't know what to do about my family," he said softly. "There is no way I can pay the bail."

Others told me, "Do not worry. We have been through this before. We will be all right." It was obvious I was the shaken one.

I have often marveled at the resilience of the African people. Famine, flood and persecution are their constant companions. Yet they struggle on while the world around them self-destructs. Struggle is perhaps the wrong word, for they live with peace, patience and even joy despite the most formidable circumstances. I also wondered, sarcastically to myself, how this cruelty fit with the spirit of Ramadan, the month when benevolence to the disadvantaged is encouraged and good deeds have special merit.

There are no guarantees, no consistency, no extras, pleasures or benefits. The weary people of Sudan only have the promise that it will get worse. Or will it? "Now the dwelling of God is with men, and he will live with them. They will be his people, and God himself will be with them. He will wipe every tear from their eyes. There will be no more death, or mourning, or crying or pain, for the old order of things has passed away" (Revelation 21:3-4).

Life is so much more than what we have materially, what we can touch or what we can see. We can be miserable with every pleasure at our fingertips. In recent days, it has been resounding in my heart: ONLY JESUS SATISFIES. Nothing else matters. It is all just wood, hay and stubble as I was so vividly reminded today. Let us not waste our time or our lives chasing the wind. Let us pursue and hold on to Jesus.

I write this from the comfort of a well-lit and protected bedroom. Outside my window, with only a bed perched amidst the rubble, lays a contented and penniless friend.

> "When you have Him you have all, but you have also lost all when you lose Him. *Stay with Christ*, although your eyes do not see Him and your reason does not grasp Him."
> — Martin Luther (emphasis added)

LAND OF THE HELPLESS

We have been reminded this week of how finite we are – that "No man comes, unless the Spirit draws him."

The month of Ramadan continues to roll by, the days blurring together and anticipation rising as the end draws near. Every evening after the sunset, the day's fast is broken when the imam issues the call to prayer. Fast breaking is a communal event, at least for the men. Large carpets are brought out and unrolled on the dusty street. Cushions to lean on are supplied. Men from the surrounding houses gather together, remove their shoes and lounge in the twilight. Those passing by are loudly encouraged to join in the celebration. Indeed it is difficult to refuse. Large platters of food are placed on the carpets. There are stews, curries, salads, fruit, dates, meats, yogurts, soups, breads and juices of every kind.

I participate in this time with mixed feelings. Warmly welcomed, food is stuffed into my hands by those around me. Conversation is light; the mood festive. Food is abundant and all are satisfied. After eating for about 20 minutes, hands are washed and the men gather in rows, being led in prayer by the most senior among them. I sit nearby, a silent spectator, as they prostrate themselves in unison, their white robes blurring into one in the increasing darkness. After the prayers, coffee, tea and watermelon are served. Everyone is now content and the talk turns to more serious things.

"We Muslims are the ones who truly honor Jesus," my new friend Mohammed tells me. "For we are the ones who respect him for who he really is." He goes on in monologue, describing the problems of Christianity and the merits of Islam. I eventually am able to share a little, but though our conversation is pleasant, it is evident the soil is barren.

"You are not far from being a Muslim," he tells me.

I smile and say, "You, my friend, are not far from being a Christian."

A little later I excused myself and headed home, happy for the contact, sobered by the need. Truly I can't convince or convert anyone by my effort "unless the Spirit draws him." A friend reminded me this week that the gospel is best preached from a position of weakness. Will you please pray the Holy Spirit will fill us to overflowing so that he spills over?

"Unless the Spirit draws him." The truth is, the Spirit IS drawing now more than ever. This Wednesday night, known as the "Night of Power," is special for Muslims. It is believed to be the day when the Koran came down from heaven by special revelation. Many Muslims will pray all night for special needs or revelation. Here in Sudan and all over the world, Christians will also be praying all night. Will you consider joining us?

LAND OF EFFICIENCY

I was on a throwback bus the other day on my way to market. It had the big rounded front fenders you see in old movies about Central America. The driver sat in the middle of the front, pushed back a little from the windshield, with passengers seated on both sides of him. The sole decoration was a baby's orange plastic sandal, nailed with a large screw to the front of the bus.

As the journey progressed, I glanced at the speedometer and noted with alarm that we were barreling along at 80 miles per hour. This was unusual because a) the bus must have been over 40 years old, b) we were stopped at a stoplight and c) the odometer read 00000002 kilometers. Not bad, I thought to myself. This miracle bus has clipped along at 80 miles per hour for 40 years and only accumulated two kilometers total mileage. Now that is efficient!

Buses are not the only efficiency marvel. We are drawing to the close of Ramadan. The city is now dead as the population fasts, or at least pretends to fast. Around 5:30 in the evening, you can sense the excitement build as sunset approaches and the daily breaking of the fast draws near. From every direction, Sudanese bustle home, whether by car, foot or donkey. By 6 o'clock the streets are deserted. Yesterday a friend unfortunately arrived at the airport just before sunset. Just as the passengers stepped off the tarmac and into the customs line, the call to prayer sounded.

Booths were slammed shut. The new arrivals were roped off and told to sit down. All the airport staff disappeared to break the fast. The airport shut down for several hours. There was nothing to do but wait. Now that is efficient!

An old Yiddish prayer says, "I thank the Lord I was not born a woman or a dog." Most Sudanese feel the same way, at least about dogs. Dogs are both feared and hated. Every opportunity is used to attack and stone them. Sudanese dogs only have two speeds. Gear one is a fast trot, ears back, head bobbing and body weaving to avoid the stones whistling in their direction. Gear two is dead still as they're worn out from all the running. It is rare to see any other speed. Despite the local disgust for them, dogs seem to thrive in the city and packs rove the streets at night.

I was sitting on my balcony at 6:30 one morning a few days ago when I was startled by a rifle shot. After a few moments, another, and then another, each one successively closer. After about 15 shots, a police pickup came into view, loaded with policemen brandishing rifles. They were the clean-up crew that shoots all the strays. My neighbor is one of the few Sudanese who actually keeps a dog as a pet. Or should I say kept? On this fateful morning Spot was in the wrong place, and our efficient police sent him to doggy heaven. Ah well, it's a dog's life!

LAND OF THE REAL

Sudan is a land where people are not restricted by some of the niceties that we bind us in the West. For example, a Sudanese picks his nose in public with impunity. With that in mind, though my mom will probably kill me, I relate the following events. Not to be coarse but merely to pass on an aspect of life not so neatly sanitized for the comfort of all.

I was invited to attend a meeting this morning at a Pentecostal church of about 200 that serves the large Ethiopian refugee population here in Sudan. I arrived early and found a seat on the right hand side of the building. I noticed the big double doors behind the pulpit were thrown open and the pulpit itself was oddly positioned, facing the side of the church. All I could see behind the

43

door was a green fence. When the service began, the worship leader stood and faced the wall to lead. This puzzled me until I made my first trip outside and noticed that the adjacent church was also filled with people. Though the worshipers were in two different buildings, they were united in heart.

This brings me to my first trip to the outside toilet. You probably noticed the adjective "first." Yes, it was one of many. I had eaten some Sudanese food last night that violently disagreed with me. By the time the sermon began, I had made three trips to the little eastern toilet and the stock of toilet paper I had brought with me had been exhausted.

Those around me sensed I was not familiar with Amharic, probably because I was holding the songbook upside down. They provided me with a translator. Now I love translators; they are some of my favorite people for they have both rescued and amused me. This guy, however, was not in that category. His breath smelled and he was so shy that he spoke in a whispered mumble. I could not hear a thing he said so I tried to guess when I was supposed to agree and nodded my head in pretended under-standing.

It was during one of these mumbled interpretations I real-ized I was in trouble. Having already made three trips outside, I was embarrassed to make another. As I struggled to appear composed, I mentally stepped off the distance to the haven of the latrine, wondering if I could make it. I struggled valiantly but real-ized gravity was winning and I needed to make a break for it.

I excused myself for the fourth time, apologizing profusely, and headed for my haven. "I think I can, I think I can." I would have made it except it was occupied – and now so were my britches. As my good friend Ron Hanson said when faced with the same situa-tion, "It is amazing how little boxer shorts will hold!"

I headed in a waddle for the next closest toilet some distance away and was blessed to find a sink. At least some kind of rescue operation would be possible. I slipped out of the stall and hung my underwear on a nearby clothesline before heading back to church. Now I know Mormons and my mom would shudder at that but I don't think God minded.

I made it through the service and began to visit with an elder. We were in the middle of planning a date for the pastor to visit us. "So when can we come?" he asked.

"I gotta go," I replied.

And off I shuffled. "I think I can, I think I can." And I would have made it but yes, again, it was occupied.

I passed my underwear as I waddled back to the more distant toilet. They seemed to be mocking me as they flapped in the breeze. The lady who had hung up her laundry earlier was now adding to it. She looked at me waddling, she looked at the underwear on the line and she looked back at me. I thank her for not breaking into hysterics. Salvaging the last of my dignity, I picked up my head, squared my shoulders and waddled on to the toilet. I still had a problem though: my underwear was on the line, my pants were now filled and I was a long way from home. After washing my pants, I made a discovery about dark clothing: if it is ALL wet, and not just in spots, it is hard to notice, as long as you don't touch it.

And so life goes on. Some days are great and wonderful things happen but they are the exception not the norm. Other days are filled with "normal" things – things both good and bad, pleasant and otherwise. It is our joy and privilege to walk with Jesus and invite him to share in all of our days.

Muslims have it right in one sense. They don't separate the sacred from the secular, normal living. Whether it is an embarrassed amble to the closest latrine, on your knees in a secret place or in the workplace as you eat your lunch, Jesus is always there. Though we sometimes find ourselves in embarrassing predicaments, Jesus is never embarrassed by us. Can we say the same about him? If our gracious heavenly Father doesn't disavow us who are his children as we walk around in our own spiritual filth, surely we can stand up for him as he dwells in unspotted holiness.

P.S. If you never hear from me again, it is because my mom has revoked my e-mail privileges.

LAND OF PROMISE

Sudan, referred to biblically as the land of Cush (Job 28:19), has known great revival in the past. Could it be that fresh showers are forthcoming?

The first recorded missionary effort in Sudan began in 580 A.D. when the Egyptian Copt, Bishop Longjainus, arrived from Egypt. The bulk of the river valley became Christian and remained so for almost 1,000 years before yielding to the advance of Islam between the 13th and 16th centuries A.D. For 300 years the salt was missing, and not until the 19th century was it replaced. At that time the Catholic Father, Daniel Comboni and the "Gordon Memorial Mission" (CMS) began working in Sudan. In the early 20th century, the Verona Fathers, the American Mission (Presbyterian) and the Sudan United Mission joined them. In 1930, the Sudan Interior Mission (now Society for International Missions) arrived and in 1940, the African Inland Mission began its work.

These missions worked almost exclusively among the Southern Bantu and Nilotic tribes. The larger tribes such as the Dinka, Nuer and Shilluk were unreceptive, so effort was concentrated on the smaller tribes. The work was slow with little, visible progress. In 1955, the Islamic government began to increase the restrictions on missionaries, and in 1964, all the missionaries were kicked out of southern Sudan. The formerly Christian North was now 100 percent Islamic.

We recently visited some ancient pyramids out in the desert, reminders of the Christian kingdoms from centuries past. They tower over the sandy landscape, quiet and lonely, as if mourning glories of bygone days. It is sobering to think of a land once so blessed with light, now so dark. It reminds us that nothing of man endures, whether it is an empire, an economy or even an ecclesiastical system. Only things of the Spirit are eternal. Therefore we have hope.

Recently in southern Sudan, some animistic tribesmen accepted Christ as their Savior. Immediately, FIRE FELL FROM HEAVEN and consumed their idols and "spirit sticks," which had been placed around the house. In a meeting recently, a pastor from the South wept as he confessed his hatred of the Arab Northerners. He said that the Lord is giving him an incredible desire to reach out to them in love.

Over and over this testimony is repeated. "A people who dwell in darkness...shall see a great light." It is with hope that we look forward to the fulfillment of Old Testament promises:

"Cush will submit herself to God" (Psalms 68:31).

"From beyond the rivers of Cush, my worshipers, my scattered people, will bring me offerings" (Zephaniah 3:10).

LAND OF RESPONSIBILITY

Islamic Sharia (pronounced Sha-re-ah) Law currently rules the country in which we live. By definition Sharia is "the clear path to be followed" or "the road to the watering place." In reality Sharia leads to bondage and oppression. The Koran defines some penalties in Sharia Law: the cutting off of a limb for stealing, death by stoning for adultery, etc. Other penalties are derived from the life and traditions of the Islamic prophet Muhammad. One of these is the penalty for murder.

The penalty for murder here in Sudan is based on a principle called "qasaas," which means retaliation. It is similar to the Old Testament concept of an eye for an eye and a life for a life. If someone murders another, the prescribed penalty is death by execution. There is an interesting loophole for the doomed murderer. It is called "diya" and basically means blood money. The family of the victim has the right to demand the death of the criminal, but if he pays the prescribed blood price to them (here in Sudan it is 100 camels or their cash equivalent), the execution can be waived.

I was discussing the redemption principle recently with a Muslim friend. I told him that all of us are sinful, powerless to save ourselves and desperately in need of a Savior.

"You mean no one is good, not even one?" he asked.

"That is right," I replied.

"Then it is hopeless," he said

I asked my friend if he was familiar with the concept of blood money, which of course he was. I then explained that Jesus paid our blood money. We were all condemned to death with no escape when he stepped in and saved our lives by giving his. I told him that because Christ paid our debt of sin, we can have eternal fellowship with God if we will repent and believe. A deep and spiritual silence descended on us. My friend sat quietly, yet it was evident the Spirit was calling him.

After a long pause he looked piercingly into my eyes and said, "If this is true, then Christians have a tremendous responsibility. Why has no one told us?"

His question echoed in my heart and I had no answer to give him. Those on whom the light first dawned have often asked this question, or a form of it: why not sooner? How can you clutch the Bread of Life to yourself when others are starving? Deeply challenged myself, I pass the question to you, "Why has no one told them?" Muslims, Chinese, teenagers, relatives and friends all need to hear.

We hold the key. Will we throw it away while others languish in prison? Will our fear, our disobedience, our love of comfort translate into damned souls? Will we one day stand on the brink of heaven and watch our friends, our neighbors and our co-workers be led away to hell? Will we hang our head when they turn with one final backward glance and ask with their eyes, "Why didn't you tell me?"

Lord Jesus, your blood has been shed to free my friends. Will their blood now be upon me? Will they suffer eternally because I did not tell them? O precious Jesus, fill my heart and open my mouth, amputate my fear and conquer my pride, that I may tell them, that they might hear, that they might believe, that we all might rejoice together.

LAND OF A STRONG GRIP

Sometimes you should hold on and sometimes you need to let go. Living in Sudan requires both from us, just as it probably does for you. It is imperative to hold on to his hand, to stand on his promises, to believe his Word and to faithfully answer his call. It is just as necessary to let go of our wills, to release our fears and worries, and to surrender our lives. Sometimes it is easier to hold on.

An Australian man and his wife arrived a few months ago. He is in the same business as we are but we do not know him well; I pass this story on secondhand. This man, whom I will call Bob, is a Type A personality. He is aggressive, confident and self-possessed – all good qualities in context. But in Africa, sometimes you win by yielding, as those of you who have been here know.

Bob stepped out of his house this weekend to take some pictures of it. Taking pictures is a sensitive issue here, even when it's something as benign as your own home. Some police officers noticed him taking the pictures and walked over to stop him. He became quite irritated. As his volume increased, so did the ire of those confronting him. They began to arrest him and he began to violently resist. As they struggled to grab him, he clutched the fence, yelling desperately for help. A friend rushed out of the house to see the somewhat humorous picture of a white man stretched through the air horizontally, two hands fastened on the fence with a policeman pulling on each leg.

We feel the same way sometimes. The Arabic language is a rascal and we desperately clutch the fence of our sanity while the bullies of discouragement and frustration yank at our legs. We are not letting go, however, and every once in a while we even muster a resistant yell.

This country is also fiercely in the grip of the Evil One. He doesn't want to let go either. But if you look closely, you will see his palms are beginning to sweat and his hold is slipping. Please continue to pray for Sudan. It really seems we are on the edge of something great in the spiritual dimension.

In an adaptation of the familiar exhortation: May you have the determination to hold on, the obedience to let go and the wisdom to know which to do when.

LAND OF GJHRUISWXXV

Gjhruiswxxv is a long-lost language of Babel. It can't be learned but it is the result of extended efforts at studying Arabic. The "symptoms" are headache, nausea and a strong desire to skip class. I wonder if my mother ever suffered from this linguistic malady? She came to America from Greece as a teenager and learned English, Spanish and later Kiswahili fluently.

My mother is a communicator. With eyes popping and hands waving, she dynamically gets her message across. She even laughs uproariously at her own jokes. Her malapropisms and mixing of metaphors, however, have long been a source of amusement to us. No metaphor is safe. Whether the subject is herself or others, animate or otherwise, all are open to misuse, adaptation and confusion. Here are some samples:

ON ANIMALS:
Our dumb cat thinks she's an animal.
Look at those immigrating birds!
How do you spell "hawk" as in "The Incredible Hog"?

ON ANATOMY:
He looks at them out of the whites of his eyes.
She always hits the jackpot on the head.
The left foot of my mouth is hurting.
I'm severing my last bite.
I fell down and hurt my uncle.
Don't feather my ruffles up!

Not only are animals and body parts get confused; locations and sources have a funny way of acquiring new meanings, assessments of character take on a new twist and suggestions get confused.

ON LOCATIONS:
That is his old stumping grounds.
We are going to find the gold at the end of the railroad.
Just a throw stones away.
We both jumped out of the table.

PART ONE

ON CHARACTER:
He knows which side his plate is buttered on.
He does not hold a shoe-latchet compared to you.
That is not a Christian song. It is circular.
She does not drop slops, I mean eye drops, I mean eavesdrops.

SUGGESTIONS:
Pictures. Do not bent!
Buy something to stack your stuffings with.
Why don't you make a "teeter-totter" casserole?

Sometimes she knows what she has said is not quite right, and though she really hustles to correct it, she still comes up a little short. "You should have seen your dad and uncle George. They were like peas in a pot. I mean two Petes in a pot. I mean two pots in a Pete." Perhaps the true mark of genius is exemplified by this last example. Any casual mixer of metaphors can confuse two sayings. Only the elite can seamlessly combine three. You have heard of the following: "a chip on his shoulder," "a bee in her bonnet "and "something against me." My mother's condensed and clarified version states: "That lady has a chip in her bonnet against me!"

As we continue to struggle with the language-learning process, we look forward to the day when we too can be laughed at, as we mix our own metaphors in Arabic.

LAND OF STUBBORN CASUALNESS
In this intriguing place, the above-mentioned characteristics are somehow seamlessly woven together. Sudanese can be stubborn. A few weeks ago, two men arrived at an intersection at the same time. One man desired to turn and the other to proceed straight ahead. Both men began to inch into the intersection, assuming the other would give way. It soon became obvious, however, that neither one was going to yield. With eyes locked on each other, they slowly and unblinkingly collided with each other in the middle of the intersection.

Sudanese can also be frustratingly casual. One of the most common words is the word "maleesh." It basically means, "never mind," "sorry" or "don't worry about it." Two men began arguing and the arguing led to blows. The blows led to knives and the knives led to bloodshed. One man was stabbed in the stomach, and the other was cut badly on his head. When the passion subsided, the first man looked at the other, shrugged and said, "Maleesh."

The other sheathed his weapon. "Maleesh," he responded.

Because of the bloodshed, however, the men were taken before a judge. "Maleesh," said the first man.

"Maleesh," said the second man.

"Maleesh," said the judge and they all lived happily ever after.

On the one hand in Sudan there is a casual and fatalistic attitude. Whatever will be, will be. Life plods along with heavy footsteps and nothing much either motivates or disturbs the people. At other times, there is stubbornness, whether of action, belief or practice. Neither the casual nor the stubborn attitudes are easily altered and in fact, they seem to merge into each other in certain instances.

This practical mindset carries over into the spiritual realm. The Islamic religion that is practiced is by and large both casual and stubborn. Most Sudanese are not fanatical Muslims or even devout ones. Yet they cling fiercely to the veneer of their religion. Their lives don't reflect their spoken beliefs, but woe to the person who dares to point out that inconsistency.

This is a strange and wonderful land. The people themselves reflect that dichotomy. Please pray we will be faithful ambassadors. Pray we will faithfully represent our stubbornly faithful King, who is not in the least bit casual in his love for these, his lost ones.

LAND OF FUTILITY

More than 300 people died in a fire in Mecca during the annual Hajj pilgrimage this week. Muslims believe Abraham set up the main mosque in Mecca after God spared his son and provided a ram. Every year over two million pilgrims make the trek to the desert, and a billion other Muslims participate in the sacrifice of a sheep at home.

A Muslim friend told us recently that every Muslim is moved to tears at the sight of the faithful massed around the Black Stone of the central mosque. And it is all in vain.

The Eid Kabir, as the holiday is known here in Sudan, lasts five days. Every family that possibly can sacrifices a sheep and eats the meat together. Wealthier friends sacrifice five sheep over the course of five days. The atmosphere is festive with extended family visiting from out of town. The men sit around playing games in their jelabas (white robes) and the women chatter happily.

These last few days have been marathon ones as we move from house to house at the invitation of our friends. From 9 a.m. until 9:30 tonight, we have been in six different homes and in each we were served drinks with huge platters of different meats, pastas, breads and desserts. One Sudanese favorite is slices of raw liver and lung mixed together with onions and a little bit of gastric juices.

Yesterday I went to the house of one of my language professors. I helped him slaughter the sheep, amazed at the speedy seconds that separate life from death. As we hung the carcass from a beam in the courtyard of his house, blood splashed on my feet and on his garment. You can see pools of blood throughout the streets of this town, a silent reminder of sacrifice. As we skinned the animal, I explained to Abdullah the story of Abraham and his answer to Isaac's question, "God himself will provide a lamb." I then told him of John the Baptist and the prophetic exclamation, "Look, the Lamb of God, who takes away the sin of the world." I explained that we Christians don't sacrifice any more, since Jesus' death did for us what repeated sacrifices couldn't do.

Abdullah was silent for a while as he continued to work on skinning the animal. Finally he said, "I think that is the difference between you and us. Your sacrifice took place once and we have to do ours over and over again.

I wish I could tell you that Abdullah immediately fell on his knees and became a Christian. But it hasn't happened yet. We have been surprised at the open doors we have had to share the gospel but sobered at the level of response. We sometimes mistakenly think that if only they can hear, they will respond. The telling and the hearing are important but there is no rebirth without the Holy Spirit. How aware we are of the futility of words alone. How desperately we need the Holy Spirit to work in the hearts of our friends.

Please pray for the Sudanese we love increasingly. Please pray the Holy Spirit will call them and they will respond. Please pray we might be faithful stewards, little candles that point to the light.

The pilgrimage is futile. The sacrifice is futile. Was the witness futile? I don't think so. Rather little seeds are nestling down into the empty corners of a dry heart. These seeds, together with your prayers, our continued relationship, and HIS watering will grow and bloom in due season.

LAND OF TIME

Sudan seems to be a land both outlasting time and trapped in it. As timeless as the great Nile River that runs from south to north and as fleeting as the infrequent refreshing of the autumn rains, Sudan remains the same. Yet it is ever changing. Sudanese are caught between the gears of placid existence and the frustration of an unstable world. Things are both forever new and still as they were.

We too feel this urgency and sluggishness. A kilometer south of our house sits an open market. Spices and trinkets, hardware and tools, drinks and refreshments, clothes and utensils are piled up under makeshift shelters. Shoppers meander elbow to elbow in the crowded market searching for needed items. Men in white robes and turbans tend the stalls. Many lay lazily in the shade of their booths or under a table of goods, seemingly without a care in the world.

The bustle of commerce is interrupted by a shrill sound of an arrogant whistle. The call to prayer approaches and a man walks through the market blowing lustily on his miniature instrument. Shoppers complete their purchases and head for the gates of the market. The market will be closed during prayers. The shopkeepers also cover their wares and head for the exits. The devout ones head for the mosque; the others squat on their haunches in small groups, idly talking.

Minutes later the whistle blower again walks through the market with a whip, lashing all who have lingered too long. (There is more than one way to increase Sunday school attendance!) When prayers are finished and the last echo from the minaret dies away, a whistle sounds and merchants and shoppers shuffle back to their respective positions.

Some day soon the greatest whistle is going to sound. Our time will be over. In the heat of the day, in the lack of responsiveness, in the frustrations of daily living, it is easy to forget the urgency of the task. It is easy to forget that our lives and times are finite.

Jennifer's close friend from Algeria recently left for home and never returned. She had not yet accepted Christ. Will she ever? She heard the good news; she received a copy of the Bible. She saw the difference between the turmoil in her home and the peace in ours. The choice is now hers. Our fleeting time with her has now passed.

We do not know how much longer we have. Life and time would dictate delay and lethargy; that is not an option for us. We all have friends, loved ones and co-workers who are running out of time. We are their watchmen. Let us do our duty.

LAND OF HISTORY

We returned this week from a conference in a country to the east. It was refreshing to leave for a couple of weeks and we were encouraged. There are no direct flights between Sudan and the country we visited due to bad relations between the two, so we flew through Egypt to get there. We spent a couple of days in the bustling metropolis of Cairo. Compared to Sudan, Cairo felt like Chicago.

The highlight of those few days in Cairo for me was a trip to an Egyptian museum. The government has opened up a mummy exhibit in recent years. In a dark, climate-controlled room, you can peer into the face of time. Pharaohs from earlier days lay preserved, somber and lifeless. You can still see their features, their hair, their skin and their fingernails. Your mind wonders and wanders back through time.

By far the most provoking of the mummies was Ramses II. This is the Pharaoh of Exodus fame – the very one which experienced the plagues, hardened his heart and lost his oldest son in the first Passover. As I pressed my face down above the glass, inches above the mummy, the Bible suddenly came alive. Here I was, inches away from the body of a man who played a pivotal role in biblical history. I will long remember that moment. I felt the same as a young child who said as he left that room, "Wow! That man talked to Moses and Moses talked to God." This was a reminder again that history is really HIS story.

This land of Sudan is not without some tales of its own. Six hundred years ago this was a God-fearing land. The many references in the Bible to Cush and Ethiopia refer to Sudan. At one time the truth was known and the light unhindered. Though it is not so now, we believe it will be again.

"Cush will submit herself to God" (Psalm 68:31).

"From beyond the rivers of Cush, my worshipers, my scattered people, will bring me offerings" (Zephaniah 3:10).

We have rivers and we have scattered people. One fine day the people of Sudan will submit themselves to God!

LAND OF TRAVEL

Sudan is a vast land of more than a million square miles. Its boundaries encompass forest, swamps, savannas, deserts and mountains. It is both an enchanting and formidable place. Some books describe it as "Africa's last frontier."

Last week we finished our last Arabic exam for the school year. We now have two months off from formal language study. We plan to use the time to do our best Joshua and Caleb imitation. We are off to check out the giants, the grapes and the milk and honey. We leave for a village in the desert this Saturday morning. Our means of transport is an old, seven-ton truck that has been fitted out to cross the barren sands. Seats have been placed in the back. There is a roof with a framework but no windows. Both the sun and the sand have free access. Our journey will take 12 hours, if all goes well. We will need to take plenty of water and probably a little food.

There are many giants in this land but all are defenseless against a sling and a little bit of faith. Please pray for us as we travel these next few months. This first trip takes us north. We then will go west and finally east. Please pray our Father will guide and protect us. Please pray he will lead us to open hearts and minds. Please pray that he turns a few heads.

On the bus home yesterday I was reading, ironically enough, a copy of Homer's Odyssey. Engrossed in the epic, I didn't notice my bus stop until almost too late. I hurriedly threw the book into the floppy briefcase on my lap and started to make my way off the bus. The man sitting in front of me was wearing the traditional white robe called a jelaba. On his head was a turban carefully wrapped with the end trailing down his back. In my haste to zip up my satchel, I zipped his turban into it.

As I tried to step off the bus, I found my progress strangely impeded. I looked behind me to find white linen connecting me to the poor man whose neck was now bent at an extreme angle. I was mortified and he was less than pleased.

Obviously, that is not the kind of head turning we aim for but I think you know which kind we want. Thank you for helping us get here. Thank you for helping us stay. Thank you for helping us turn their heads the Right way.

LAND LIKE MARS

Yes, yes, I know there is great excitement in the realm of science over the exploration of this unknown and difficult planet, but the wildness of Mars can't have much over the bewildering world through which I travel.

Thanks to the generosity of youth groups in the United States, we were able to purchase a new car last week. It has been a tremendous blessing already, apart from the registration process.

Registration takes place with the Sudan traffic police. They have two centers, roughly two kilometers apart. During the registration process, I added 40 km to the odometer. The first stage was relatively painless. I obtained a blank form from a policeman sitting at the front gate. I then turned around to the numerous "filler-outers" who would fill in the form. I went inside to an official who inspected my driving license then back outside to a man who inspected my car's engine and chassis number, back to the policeman at the gate for his signature, back to the official inside for his stamp of approval, back outside to a small booth for a different stamp, back inside to a large room crammed with desks. At each desk, a tax was paid and my form scribbled on. These taxes included a road and bridge tax, a poor tax (for the unfortunate), a war tax (for the jihad), a sugar tax (for who knows what) and several others I can't remember. I went back outside to the policeman at the gate and stage one was finished. That was the easy part.

Stage two began in the police headquarters. An application form was filled out and initialed by the superior. I was then taken past a slew of offices, through two small restaurants, around several tight corners, down an alley, to an office on the dark side of the establishment. There another officer filled out a second form and sent me back to the original officer for another signature and stamp. From there I went to a small window to pay, then a second window and another tax, then another signature from the office on the dark side. After that, the fun really began.

The car license can't be issued until the license plates are made. (A private company makes the license plates.) It couldn't make the license plate until the police issued the license plate number. The police wouldn't issue the number because the license plate makers were on strike. The license plate makers were on strike because the police hadn't paid them in months.

The officer in charge shrugged and said, "It is easy. Just drive to the company and see if they will agree to make you one. Then drive back here and we will tell you what your number should be. Then drive back to them and tell them the number. Then drive back to us and we will give you the car license."

Off we went to plead our case to the unpaid strikers. We met a policeman at the door and he offered to help us. We drove off to the company, but no dice. No license plate either. Back at the police headquarters the officer said, "Don't worry, we might be able to get one for you in a month."

We were headed out when we met another officer. He said, "Come with me. I know the chief of police for all Sudan."

We were led back into the guts of the complex. We passed office after office. I saw a lot of newspapers, heads collapsed on desks and even beds for little naps. One of the offices was carefully designated "Secret Office." It makes you wonder. Five minutes with this chief, a quick telephone call and we had our license plate number. We sped off to the company, happily paying six times the usual price. I watched them make the license plate and paint it, and then bustled back to headquarters.

Back at headquarters, I had to turn in all of our paperwork – all receipts, all records, all originals, even the title deed. This made me a little nervous, especially when they refused to issue a receipt. "Tomorrow, if God wills!" was the only comment.

Well, God must have willed. The next morning I went back and they had lost my paperwork. After a lazy search and the addition of two ulcers to my system, the papers turned up again. A couple more offices, a couple more rubber stamps, a couple more signatures, and presto! We were official.

Yes, Mars has nothing on Sudan. The whole exercise has been educational. I am devising a similar system – complete with application forms, multiple offices, numerous rubber stamps and endless required signatures – for anyone who wants to use our bathroom.

Don't forget that five minutes with the Chief makes all the difference. In the spiritual realm, how often do we run around aimlessly, when a few quiet minutes with the King would answer everything?

LAND OF INTRIGUE

Many of you know that we are attending two language schools. The language program in the university that is responsible for our visas is poor. We attend classes there in the afternoons to validate our visas and attend a private school in the mornings where our real learning takes place.

This week marks the end of our year visa. We needed a letter from the university to apply for a new one at the Foreign Affairs Department. The professor in charge kindly helped us. Two days ago he called our house in the morning and said, "The letters are ready. They are in a file on my desk. Go ahead and get them yourself. I won't be in today."

I headed to the university and explained the situation to a secretary. We scouted around for the file and found it. The top papers were our required letters. As I was putting them in my briefcase, an official stormed in, screamed at the secretary, snatched the papers from me, slammed them back in the file and angrily ordered us out. I tried to talk to him but he just left me standing outside. The secretary shrugged and melted away. I was in a dilemma. Our visas would run out in a few days and I couldn't re-apply without those papers. I walked around thinking, "Maybe I can talk to this man and explain the situation." I tried to find him but gave up and rationalized that a James Bond maneuver was in order.

I snuck back to the office and let myself in quietly. I felt like an intruder in Stalin's Kremlin. With heart pounding and nerves tingling, I found the file, grabbed the papers, stuffed them in my briefcase and dashed for the exit. Within yards of the door, a voice stopped me and my heart sank. I turned to find a different professor wanting to greet me. Doesn't the Lord have a sense of humor?

Later that day, I was back at the university for a class. As I was leaving, I saw the official who had expelled me waiting for a bus with some colleagues. I stopped and offered them a ride. The man would have refused but his friends jumped in and beckoned him to follow. He sheepishly got in the front seat next to me. I offered him my hand and gave him a big smile. He relaxed a little as I drove to the bus station and chatted in Arabic as if nothing had ever happened. God is good.

Eric Hoffer said, "It is easier to love humanity as a whole than to love one's neighbor." It is easy for me to get warm fuzzies when I think in general terms about Muslims. When it comes to certain individuals, if they are proud, difficult, vengeful or hard, I suddenly find the warm fuzzies disappear and the difficult reality of the mercy life becomes apparent. When I get screamed at, when the Muslim convert I am studying the Bible with makes fun of my Arabic day after day, or when the same guy keeps stealing from me, I realize how deceived I am. The reality of loving difficult people needs the unnatural love of Christ.

LAND OF NAMES

Sudanese names are similar to those in other Arab countries. Each child takes the name of his father, his grandfather and his great-grandfather, etc., for as far back as they can remember. There are no family names, just a succession of first names. For example, my name would be Dick Richard Claude Matthew etc. On passports or other documents, only the four most recent names are listed. A woman's name does not change after marriage, she keeps the name of her father for life. For example, if we had a daughter Grace, she would be called Grace Dick Richard Matthew. This sounds funny to the Western ear. (Speaking of sounding funny, Dick means rooster in Arabic. At least it's not toad or cockroach!)

I like this system of naming for the continuity it suggests. In our individualized society, we are losing the sense of belonging to extended family. Not only are we more removed from each other's victories and joys, we are also more detached from one another's sorrow and failure. I like the fact that "we keep the name of the Father for life." We are his children, called by his name (Revelation 14:1). And in an ironic and glorious twist the Father became flesh and took our name, man.

Names and the concepts behind them have been on the brain recently after we were invited to a naming ceremony this week. This takes place a week after the baby's birth. Sheep are slaughtered and their blood is symbolically shed to ensure protection over a child. In fact, in any major acquisition, blood should be applied to protect against evil.

We purchased a new car recently. Our Sudanese friends insisted we slaughter a sheep and smear blood on the sides to protect the car from demons and the evil eye. We explained that we live under the blood of Jesus and did not need any other blood. "What about us?" they asked. I told them Jesus would protect them in our car and they relaxed. What I should have said is, "You need to live under the blood of Jesus too!"

We are amazed at the opportunities the Lord brings our way to apply scriptural truth. Pray with us, for we really need the fullness of the Spirit to be a constant witness. Every day I am reminded of the difference between what I believe and what I want to believe. I believe Jesus is the only way. When I see the millions upon millions headed steadily towards hell, my emotions want to believe something else. I can either despair or be jolted awake and realize Jesus is coming SOON! For me that is great; for others it is lethal. May we be stirred to prayer, to action, to doing our part, so countless Sudanese will have HIS blood applied to their lives and their names changed to Mohammed Ahmed Redeemed Child of God!

LAND OF SHEEP

Sudan supposedly has enough resources to be the breadbasket of the Middle East. While it is true that the north is largely desert, the center and south of the country have ample rain. In the immense triangle formed by the confluence of two rivers, there are huge irrigation schemes. Further south are endless grasslands where cattle and sheep abound, at least when they are not getting shot or blown up by land mines.

A sheep attended our meeting last night. I was speaking at a conference for Christian university students being held in a run-down club. We were sitting outside with rabbits and sheep as company. As we waited for the service to begin, Jennifer started laughing. I turned to find a large ewe rubbing its head on her foot. The ewe then ambled down the long aisle, looking as much at home as any member of the throng. A few minutes later, the choir began singing on the stage. Our friend the sheep, wanting to be helpful, climbed up on the stage and attempted to join in the vocal ministry. I wondered how she would respond when I gave the altar call.

Sudan is a land of sheep in other ways. The people of this great land have suffered so much that they don't know where to turn. The following is taken from a recent news report:

"Riot police had to be sent to the main prison on July 31, to forcibly evict people whose prison terms had come to an end. About 1,200 convicts who were due for release that day, including 74 women granted amnesty by the President, refused to leave the prison. A daily newspaper quoted some prisoners as saying they were unwilling to leave because they no longer knew the whereabouts of their relatives, while others were afraid they would not be able to manage in the outside world."

Another report disclosed:

"According to a report published here in the capital, more than 300 teachers sent abroad for graduate studies...have refused to return home. This represents a loss of more than 80 percent of the staff sent for studies abroad."

It is not easy being a sheep, especially a Sudanese one. Despite all the social and economic problems, however, the most tragic affliction is spiritual. Countless flocks are wandering aimlessly without the Shepherd. If the Eternal Shepherd willingly left the 99 in the fold and looked for the lost one, how much more, here in Sudan, he is seeking the 99 who are lost!

LAND OF DREAMS

Miriam walked into the crowded hospital for the fourth time that week to visit her cousin who had been bedridden for months. Miriam had been witnessing to her cousin for some time. She realized, during her trips to the hospital, that an old man who lay near her cousin was obviously dying and obviously without peace. Miriam began to spend time with him, telling him the story of the Crucified. One day as she walked to the familiar dirty room, she was met by the sound of mourning. The old man had passed away. His granddaughter pulled Miriam aside and whispered, "He became a Christian just before he died. He died in such peace. I want to know more."

Miriam, a former Muslim, became a Christian a few years ago. Last year her husband, Mabrook, followed. They get up in the middle of the night to study the Bible while the rest of their family sleeps. The King often talks to them in dreams and visions.

Miriam's cousin also became a Christian. When her family found out, they were furious, determined to marry her off to an old fundamentalist Muslim. Miriam did not know what to do. One night in a dream she saw herself get on a specific bus with this young cousin and head off into the desert.

After prayer and counsel, she felt the dream was indeed from the Lord. She snuck to this girl's house in the middle of the night. The girl climbed over the wall and they boarded the bus and set off together into the unknown. Their first stop was with a distant relative of Miriam's husband, Mabrook. All went well until it was time to pray.

"Let's all pray," the relative said.

"NOT US!" said the young girl, "We are now followers of Jesus!"

Eyes widened and mouths dropped, and even more so Miriam's who had been keeping this secret from her family. The welcome ended and the two found themselves on the street in a strange town, far from home and knowing no one.

God is good, however, and a stranger approached them on the street. "You look tired!" he said. "Come home with me to meet my mother and rest."

The mother asked no questions and welcomed them into the home. After several days, she embraced the young girl saying, "You are like my daughter; I want you to live with me!" Miriam returned home, alone and happy.

The husband Mabrook has also had the Lord speak to him. Traveling in the west with six of his cattle-herding clansmen, he began to tell them about the truth. Mabrook is the only known Christian from his tribe. His friends became intrigued by what he shared with them.

One day, six cows were lost and the herders became frantic. The loss would be their responsibility to repay. "Mabrook, can you pray for us?" they asked.

He did. That night in a dream, the Lord showed him exactly where the cows were and how to get there. In the morning he led the men directly to the lost cows. The men were overcome with thanks and curiosity.

They plan to visit the capital this month to meet with Mabrook and learn more about his wonderful Savior. Plans are being made to show them the Jesus film.

Sudan is a land of dreams, a land of reality. What HE is beginning to do here is real. We look forward with great anticipation to what is in store! Thank you for anticipating with us.

LAND OF FULFILLMENT

Time can march, pass, stretch, speed, stop, stand, whirl and everything in between. In Sudan it seems to glide, almost imperceptibly connecting the past to the present and the present to the future. Aspects of dress and certain customs have remained unchanged for centuries while satellite dishes, cell phones and the Internet are readily available. In some countries I have noticed more of a distinction, but here, I don't know, maybe it is the heat frying our brains, contradictions are easier to swallow and paradoxes blur together.

I was sitting in a Sudanese house recently listening to an old sermon tape of Billy Graham speaking to young people at an Urbana conference, challenging them to missions. His anointed message was relevant to 1997. I was moved and motivated. Imagine my surprise when he mentioned in passing that the year was 1957. Forty years ago and it seemed like yesterday. I did a quick calculation and realized my dad was 16 years old at that time. Was it in a service like that that his heart was first stirred to missions?

I mention my dad because of this sense of history. A light is beginning to dawn that truly the Master Planner is at work as our life glides on in Sudan. We are not here by accident or by our own design. Fifteen years ago, my dad made his first visit to Sudan. The following is an excerpt from his 1982 newsletter:

> "As the midday sun turned me red like a lobster, I wondered what is the future for Sudan? Very dark and bleak in the natural, but catching a small glimpse of what God wanted and was about to do, I rejoiced in my heart for that tremendous spiritual awakening that was beginning to spread in southern Sudan. By God's mercy, may it also break the hearts of the Arabs in the north and may thousands of Muslims turn to Christ."

We are not in Sudan to fulfill my dad's unfinished dream. In fact, he really did not want us to come here. Yet God in his wisdom connects plowing to planting, planting to watering, watering to pruning and pruning to harvest. Ultimately, in his time God will bring the increase. We are not a solitary pawn in either the history of this nation or the strategy of God to reach it. We are intricately connected – even with some we may not be aware of – in a wonderful harvest scheme. Through time, transitions, disappointments, opposition and even through harm, the standard steadily moves forward and God's plan glides on. Thank you for playing your part in this unfinished wonder.

LAND THAT IS BROKEN

It was a day like any other. The routine of life had become an opiate and I drifted from task to responsibility in a dream-like state. I was not being lazy; I was not shirking responsibility; I was not wasting time. I was merely dulled by the familiar. I had become so used to my environment that I no longer saw it clearly. I suppose this happens to everyone, everywhere, yet Sudan has a knack for waking you up.

I boarded the crowded transport and settled down on the hard wooden bench. The man across from me looked normal enough. His clothes were old and faded, and his eyes tired and hopeless. His hands rested on his lap, or should I say hand. His left hand had been severed at the wrist and he now covered it with a ragged, brown sock. He was a reminder that this land lives under the strain of strict Islamic law and the punishment for stealing is the severing of a hand.

Later that night I sat in the house of a former Muslim as he related his testimony of how he had come to Christ. Furious relatives snatched his beautiful young wife and child from him. He now lives alone and jobless in a threatening world. I realized again that we live in a land that is broken.

The speed at which our senses are dulled is alarming. It does not take long, even in the midst of tremendous suffering and loss, to lapse into a hazy fog of indifference. There are plenty of excuses I suppose, but none of them valid. And then in the midst of our apathy, routine and ignorance, HE sends a little message and the light blinks on again. Sometimes it is a severed hand; sometimes it is a heart-rending story. Sometimes it is a song, a poem or a scripture verse. Sometimes it is a rainbow, a cloud or a mountain. Sometimes it is the life of a friend, the example of a mentor or the tear of a child. Sometimes it is a glimpse into the selfishness of our own hearts.

I don't want to forget! I don't want to forget that almost everyone I know is headed for a Christless eternity. I want to remember the routine is the means and not the end. I want to be constantly aware that Jesus is coming and we have a lot of going, discipling, baptizing and teaching yet to do. I want to be motivated by a broken world not paralyzed by it.

LAND OF OIL

The buzz on the street and through the offices here in the capital is all about oil. Oil has supposedly been discovered in the North and West. Optimists are saying Sudan will become the new Kuwait. Pessimists grumble that the rich will just get richer and the poor will continue to be miserable. The jury is still out, as is the oil. Several kinds of it, in fact.

Last week we went with some friends to visit a Sudanese family. They are Muslims but several of us have made some good contacts with them over time. The wife, an older woman, was recently diagnosed with inoperable cancer and the whole family has been shaken. In a surprising step, we were invited to come to their house and pray for her.

We arrived under cover of darkness and slipped into the small compound. We were worried that several foreigners together in such a place would attract undue attention. As we sat in the courtyard under the stars, we had a quiet conversation together. One of us read from James 5: "Is any one of you in trouble? Is any one of you sick? He should call the elders to pray over him and anoint him with oil."

Tea had been brought but it sat forgotten. We explained the symbolism of oil and then anointed the woman and prayed for her. It was a blessed time. A few minutes after we finished praying, she simply said, "I am not afraid anymore!"

For several days, this Muslim lady refused to wash the oil off her forehead. She told her daughters, "I have more faith in those prayers than in the doctor's medicine."

Please continue to pray for this Sudanese family and countless others like them. They still have not joined the body of Christ but are steadily being wooed by their gentle Lover. Please pray the Father will continue to pour out his oil, just like the Good Samaritan did to the man he found bleeding and dying on the Jericho road. He poured on the oil and the wine.

LAND OF RESCUE

I went with Bashir to the swimming pool this week. He is an Algerian diplomat who is a Muslim but a carnal one. Over the last year and a half, his wife and Jennifer have become close friends. We have good fellowship with them and have even given them a Bible.

As Bashir and I sat watching the children swim, it suddenly dawned on us that one was flailing desperately in the water. Fortunately the child was near the side of the pool and we were able to pull him out.

We had no sooner finished that rescue than two more children panicked in the deep water and started to drown each other in their attempt to stay afloat. Unfortunately, I am not Superman and there was no telephone booth near by, so I had to go in fully clothed. The girls were hysterical and had swallowed a lot of water, but everything turned out okay. I was laughed at as I walked out to the car, dripping wet, but the thrill of saving a life was awesome.

Other souls are also drowning. They too need a hand into the lifeboat. You live next to them, you are related to them, you love them and you see them every day. They are your spouse, your friend, your boss and your co-worker. Here in Sudan it is uncomfortable to consider that all of our friends, all of our teachers, our landlord, the men in the market we buy from – practically everyone we know – are flailing away in the deep end of deception and going down for the third time.

It is not often you get to save a life. It is not often you see the giant tumble. It is not often the hardened repent. It is not often the fire falls. It is not often the dead are raised. But it happens. It happens because we pray. It happens because we believe. It happens because we are there. It happens because we obey. In these last days, the "not often" is about to become the routine. Let us pray! Let us believe! Let us be there! Let us obey!

LAND OF TOMATO CANS

We all know you have to be somewhat careful with tomato cans.

They can fall off a shelf and dent themselves on our heads. They can bust through shopping bags and cushion their fall on our toes. They can even wickedly slice our fingers with their serrated edges. These dangers are common but in Sudan there is a more sinister threat.

The power of the curse continues to play a role in the lives of everyday Sudanese people. If one has a problem with a friend, neighbor or relative, the ways to curse them are legion. A favorite one is to go to a holy man (!) and have him write out a curse. The curse is then placed in a tomato can and secretly buried in the yard of the disfavored one.

Mabrook and Miriam are a young Christian couple that converted from Islam. Their neighbors started to experience all kinds of sickness and problems. Everything started to go wrong and they even felt an oppressive spirit in their house.

One night in a dream, the Lord revealed to Mabrook and Miriam that there was a curse buried in a tomato can in their neighbor's yard. As soon as they could, when the neighbors had left the house, they snuck in and found the buried curse and destroyed it.

The very next day the neighbors came to visit and happily reported, "Something has changed! We feel so free in the house!"

Here in Sudan there is great bondage and deception. Many Sudanese live in fear and suspicion. Please pray God will break through these chains. Please pray that Mabrook and Miriam will be used in this situation to be proclaimers. Please pray for their protection as they are facing attacks from many directions. Please pray all of us will live under the shelter of the blood and be protected from the power of the curse.

This Sunday we leave for an exploratory trip in the East. We are visiting a region that is difficult to access. Please pray God will watch over us and lead us to the right people – a Muslim people-group with more than three million people, spread over three countries with only three known Christians. For you mathematicians, that equals 0.00001 percent of the people (one thousandth of one percent). May he help us!

LAND OF PERMISSION

We returned two days ago from a trip to eastern Sudan. Happy, but tired and sick, we were glad to be home. The trip was very informative and will help us as we pray about our next step. Getting there was challenging. Because Sudan has a terrible relationship with its northeastern neighbor, travel to that region is restricted and difficult. Before even leaving the capital here, travel permission must be obtained from security.

As soon as we arrived at the airport, more officers met us to check our papers. In town we registered with the security office before we could check into a hotel. To visit any area of town, we had to get clearance from security. To go snorkeling in the sea, we had to get permission. To leave town, we had to get clearance. On the bus ride home, we were stopped over 16 times on a 1,000-kilometer stretch of road. Sometimes they searched our luggage, sometimes they examined our passports, they always scribbled their approval on our worn-out travel permits. Everything had to be approved. We almost started to ask permission to use the restroom, or should I say, rest bush.

Though the constant checks became wearisome, they caused me to think about my obedience to the Lord. The "it is easier to ask forgiveness rather than permission" principle often applies to my life. It is so easy for me to think up grand schemes, plan great exploits, begin far-reaching projects and only afterwards slip the design under God's door in hope of "the rubber stamp" of his approval. I often end up needing to ask his forgiveness.

As you pray for us, please pray we will only do his will. It is so easy to do every other thing, ANY other thing, than his will. With twisted motives, selfish goals and lack of wisdom, we often stumble about in our frenzied efforts to build the Kingdom and end up in a tangled mess, blaming co-workers, organizational structures, cultural differences, language problems or lack of resources. In short, we blame everyone but ourselves.

Please forgive us for the times we do the wrong thing. Please forgive us for the times we do the right thing for the wrong reasons. Please forgive us when we do the right thing for the right reasons at the wrong time. We are very conscious of being good stewards of your support and God's time, and yet we often miss the mark. We really only want to do his will. Thank you for praying with us about this problem. "Though I give my body to be burned, but have not love, it profits me nothing..." (1 Corinthians 13:3).

LAND OF TECHNOLOGY

A security official claimed Israel is using swans to spy on Sudan. He said some swans, flying over Sudan on their seasonal migration, were found to have electronic tags and tiny cameras attached to their feet.

Speaking on national television the State Defense Minister, equally defiant, warned that no one in Sudan would escape military service. He said he plans to recruit more than two million soldiers before the end of 1997. He also warned parents not to hide their children. He said special forces have been set up to hunt for those who try to dodge the call-up. The campaign has been stepped up with roadblocks in the major towns. Officials patrol the streets with loudspeakers, urging parents to hand over their children. Young people are being seized on the streets and in public places or pulled from private cars and public transport vehicles and trucked off to military training camps without notifying their families.

You never know what to expect in Sudan. Swans loaded with cameras, cars patrolling the streets with loud speakers looking for children to send to the front lines as cannon fodder, or a Muslim cut to the heart by the showing of a video.

A book exhibition was held here in the capital last week. Bible literature was sold during the day and films were shown at night. This year an unprecedented number of Muslims visited both events. Last week a dignified Muslim in flowing robe and turban attended a showing of the Jesus film. He sat in rapt attention for the duration of the video. When the film concluded, he remained rooted to his chair with his head bowed. For 30 minutes he did not move. Eventually someone went over to talk to him. Tears were streaming down both of his cheeks. Overcome with emotion, he was not able to talk. Slowly he got up and walked out of the room.

From our fourth floor apartment balcony, we can see more than a dozen satellite dishes. The government allows a Christian program to air one hour a week on national television. These Bible expositions are unheard of in most Muslim nations. Incredible amounts of biblical literature have been distributed. Hearts are hungry; dry souls are thirsty.

Muslims ARE reachable. Please continue to pray for them. Please pray for every tool and medium of communication being used. Please pray the seeds being sown will fall on good soil, and the ones who cry after watching the story of the King will invite him into their hearts.

LAND OF CRISIS

Most of you have probably been following the developments in Iraq – threats, expulsions, angry words and politicking. The networks all covered the story, each one positioning for the best angle. Though our media is detailed, it is selective. The crises that arise and fade are often inconsequential to the spirit, minimal in the light of eternity. News of much greater import hardly ever crosses Dan Rather's desk. Cindy just arrived in Sudan last week from Iraq. Here is her story:

Saddam Hussein has an emotionally disturbed son who spends considerable time in a psychiatric hospital. One day Cindy strongly felt the Lord telling her to visit him in the hospital. The hospital is guarded. When she approached the entrance, an officer stopped her and asked, "What do you want?"

"I want to visit Saddam Hussein's son."

"On whose authority?" he demanded.

"By the authority of Jesus Christ," Cindy responded.

"Oh!" he said and swiftly picked up his walkie-talkie. "A woman is here on the authority of Jesus Christ. Let her proceed immediately!"

Cindy spent quality time witnessing to Saddam's son. At the end of her visit he said, "You are like the Good Samaritan in the

Holy Bible. Everyone else has passed me by, but you have minis-
tered to my needs."

Cindy visited another ward filled with severely afflicted
patients. In a few minutes, Cindy had them all singing a Christian
song peacefully. The staff at this Muslim hospital was amazed.
One doctor said, "Now I know Jesus Christ is all powerful! No
one else has been able to calm these patients."

Though you do not hear stories like this on the evening news,
be assured they take place. In Iraq, in Sudan, throughout the
Middle East and around the world, the Spirit is moving, calling,
inviting, inspiring, healing, redeeming and advancing. He uses
many means and all kinds of people but it is his doing and his
kingdom is being built. May we all play our part in his ultimate
plan – to redeem people from every tribe, tongue and nation.

Oh, and I want you to know that brave Cindy is a teenager.

LAND OF ROUTINE

You guess it is going to be a tough day when you wake up to the
sound of an off-key imam wailing from the top of the nearby
minaret. You are pretty sure it is going to be a rough one when
you discover your spare tire was stolen during the night. You are
convinced it is going to be a long one when by 9:30 in the morning you are totally confused in the middle of an Arabic exam. You
are resigned to your fate when as the sun sets a white-robed man
points a gun inches from your face and pulls the trigger.

The crowd was growing excited as I sat with my back against
the wall trying to blend into the group. Since there were 80 Arab
men in white robes and I was a white man in blue jeans, I didn't
really succeed. A signal, a stirring and suddenly a man rushed
up to me and pulled the trigger. My heart leapt and the gun mis-
fired. He tried again and I could only sit and stare, not thinking
the camera in my numb hands could possibly capture a historic
moment. On the third attempt, the hammer lurched down on the
shell and both of my ears popped.

Luckily for me, my mom and my life insurance company, the
gun, though only inches from my face, was pointed upwards. It

was fired to mark the sealing of a wedding ceremony. Though I missed a great picture, the good news is that one day I will probably be able to hear again.

By the time we got home, it was 10 p.m. and someone was waiting to see me. We talked until midnight and then I climbed in the pickup to drive him home. We headed out to the camp for displaced people on the outskirts of the city. It was not until we had passed the fifth army road-block and were bumping along the stony road with 14 people in the pickup and the lights of the city only a memory in my rearview mirror, that I remembered I no longer had a spare tire and I was flying to Kenya in a couple of hours. Yup, just another old boring day in Sudan.

LAND OF TIMING

Sometimes you have it; sometimes you don't. Timing. With it you make a good comedian. Without it, you make a lousy politician. Sudanese seem to fall in the latter category. I tip my hat to them, however, in the effort category. In certain cases, they really hustle, though their energy is often misguided. Let me quote from a letter recently written to a high ranking Sudanese official:

"It is with deep concern that Human Rights Watch received reports of the imminent execution on December 10, 1997, internationally celebrated as Human Rights Day, of four women convicted of prostitution in the capital. We urge your government to refrain from executing these women because doing so would violate international and U.N. human rights standards. Under these circumstances, imposing the death penalty on four women on international Human Rights Day would make a mockery of human rights.

"We also protest the detention, beating and flogging of another group of women who were demonstrating in the capital, in the exercise of their right of free expression. This penalty was carried out at 1 a.m. on December 2, 1997, within 24 hours of their arrests."

The women all received 10 lashes, except for one poor soul

with the audacity to wear pants. She received 40.

What lousy timing! We sometimes wonder where Sudan fits into the Master's timeline. Have we been forgotten? Is the "dove" descending everywhere but here? Has the Lord of Time turned his back on the Sudanese zone?

Though it would be easy to listen to the implanted doubts of the enemy, though times are trying and victories few, we still believe strongly, "NOW IS THE TIME, NOW IS THE DAY OF SALVATION!" There are opportunities in Sudan; there are unparalleled open doors in similar countries. We consider it a privilege to be here in the center of his timing.

Thanks to all of you who keep us here. Timing, for all of us, is the key – the time we spend in the Lord's presence. Thank you for meeting us there!

LAND OF SECURITY

Normally the word "security" conjures up pleasant mental pictures – thoughts of peace, quiet and safety. Normally, security assures us and denotes reliance, shelter and refuge. But Sudan is not normal.

Security here refers to a branch of authority similar to the American CIA or the Soviet KGB. They have contacts on every street corner and informers in every office. The Sudanese are scared to death of their "security."

We have a close friend, a former Muslim, whom we had the privilege of baptizing last year. A few weeks ago, he was stopped on his way home from the market. He tried to run but was quickly apprehended. He was taken into a small room and seated on a chair in front of a table. A plain-clothes officer whipped out a pistol and slammed it down in front of our friend. For 12 hours the intimidation and interrogation continued. Are you a Christian? Do you go to Christian meetings? Who are your Christian friends?

As dawn broke, a Muslim member of our friend's family who holds an important position in the military was called. "Your brother has become a Christian!" they accused.

Fortunately for our friend, his brother couldn't believe such a scandalous accusation. He managed to convince the security officer to release our friend. He was released but strongly warned to have nothing to do with Christians, Christian meetings or any association like this. Our friend is still free but deathly afraid of his "security."

Increasingly in our world we must turn to the Rock that is higher than we are. In countries like Sudan, it is evident manmade structures, supposedly created for our convenience, protection and liberation, can quickly do just the reverse. We see that blatantly in the misnomer "security." But how about convenience? How about computers? How about clutched blessings mysteriously transformed into chains? The things intended to serve us so quickly become our masters.

We feel deeply for the plight of our friend. He lives in constant danger. He has no one he can trust. Yet he retains one advantage that we, with our freedom, have lost. He lives in a black and white world. The limits are clearly defined, vibrant in their distinction. We, in our world, tend to lean towards ineffectual dullness in our colorless grey.

Let's pray for our friend but not pity him. Rather, pity us and the handicap of living in a comfortable, colorless world.

LAND OF MIXED SIGNALS

Driving in Sudan is interesting and occasionally hazardous. The bad news is rules don't exist. The good news is, unlike many countries, almost everyone drives slowly. A person might perform the most outlandish maneuver on the road but at such a geriatric pace that you have ample time to avoid him. As long as you are careful, you usually arrive at your destination without incident.

I do admit, however, that yesterday I arrived at a road junction with more than a little bewilderment. This four-way crossing was equipped with two sets of stoplights, one on either side of the road. One stoplight was a brilliant green and the other a flaming red. I was not the only one confused. Other cars traveling in the same direction encountered the same dilemma. Some obeyed the green light and moved on through the intersection; others stopped submissively for the red. Matters improved little when the lights changed, for the red became green and the green changed to red.

Sudan can be bewildering. On the one hand, there is a measure of religious freedom. The state would like the observing world to believe that there is complete freedom here. Churches are allowed to function and even large public meetings are tolerated. Recently a large "family conference" was held with 20,000 people attending on the final night, all of them from the South. But then on the other hand, a Muslim who comes to know Christ as Savior is subject to beating, mistreatment, social rejection, imprisonment and sometimes even death.

A man named Fonzy is currently in prison, charged with crimes against the state. He has been accused of making a bomb. If convicted, he could face 20 years in prison, a more favorable sentence. He could be sentenced to death. Fonzy's only crime is that he is a servant of the King – one of only three known Christians from a group of almost three million.

Why do people want to kill you when you tell them how to get to heaven? Why does the enemy so zealously guard his domain? Is he sending a mixed signal? Does he know he has lost the game but continues to claw at others to drag down with him?

The signals of our Lord are clear: I have won. I have redeemed you. I have called you by name. I am with you. I am good. I am merciful. I am eternal. I am faithful. I am the truth. I am the way. I am the life. I am. This clear, simple signal is ours to relay. Let us be faithful in that endeavor.

LAND OF SLEEP

The month of Ramadan is over and so are the three o'clock morning prayers. The last 10 nights of Ramadan are considered especially blessed and for those 10 nights from about two to four a.m., prayers are recited over the loudspeaker in the nearby mosque. Our fourth floor apartment has our bedroom window directly in line with the adversarial speaker. The first few nights we couldn't sleep as the prayers droned on in our minds. On the third night, we asked the Lord to close our ears to the sound, for it disturbed our spirits and hindered our sleep. From that night on, we slept like babies.

A lot of things happen in your sleep. My friend Scott Hanson had animated dreams in boarding school. One night we heard a thumping sound and found him perched on a dresser banging his head against the ceiling. He was dreaming he was caught in a tunnel, trying desperately to escape. Thankfully, he woke up from that nightmare. Many in Sudan are not so privileged.

A young family that I call "The Dreamers" are secret believers. Recently, Mrs. Dreamer was home alone when some relatives walked into their house unannounced. She had no time to hide some Christian literature that was lying about. The relatives went into hysterics – screaming, cursing and threatening. When the husband came home, she informed him of the trouble.

"I have bad news, too," he said. "I have been accused falsely of stealing a gun from the office." (Mr. Dreamer has a position with security. Our God has his candles everywhere!)

Mrs. Dreamer was not surprised. "I know that," she said. "God showed me in a dream you would have trouble at the office. God even showed me who would cause the trouble. I didn't tell you because I didn't want you to worry."

We are so different from these beloved friends. We have Christian roots and heritage with support systems and structures. We have countless friends and families who affirm us. We have a ticket out of here if things get rough. The Dreamers, and others like them, have none of this. No support, no Christian heritage, no encouragement. Only accusations, mistrust and hate. Yet with courage and faith, they press on through uncharted waters. Please lift them up to the Father. They desperately need your prayers.

Yesterday the vice president of Sudan and other officials died in an accident. As I watched the news, I solemnly realized time had run out for them. They have awakened from this dream we call life and must now face the nightmare of an eternity without Christ. How many others in this land of sleep will never wake up to the reality of Jesus?

May we be a shrill, clear but persistent alarm clock.

LAND OF VISIONS

Pizza, popcorn and scary movies have been known to affect one's subconscious itinerary. They often deprive you of your much longed-for repose. The Dream Giver does too, only much more effectively.

Homer is a man from a totally Muslim tribe. He has been a seeker for some time but hasn't had the courage to take that final and significant step of faith. I have written about the "Night of Power" and how Muslims pray for special insight. We too, along with some like-minded partners, were praying for Muslims that night. We each selected a specific Muslim to pray for and asked that the Dream Giver would reveal himself in a special way in the night. One of our group selected Homer.

It seems the selection was ordained. That night Homer dreamed he had passed away. Angels and demons were gathered around his body, arguing over him. The angels aspired to take him to heaven; the demons desired to drag him down to hell. In the midst of their heated argument, someone, whom both angels and demons feared, stepped in. That someone reached out and lifted Homer up, interceding for him.

"Who are you?" Homer asked.

"My name is Jesus," came the simple reply as the demons fled.

When asked later to describe Jesus, Homer said, "He had a long, flowing white robe, a dark-colored vest, brown skin and big bushy hair."

This is an exact description of someone from Homer's tribe, the Beja. There are only three believers among almost three million. Or should we make that four?

The Lord is so good. He is no respecter of persons. Red and yellow, black and white, Jesus loves the lost ones of this world. He has no favorites; he is not restricted by culture. He is not bound by one strategy and knows no limitation. Our Jesus of Nazareth is the first and the only legitimate Renaissance man. He breaks down all barriers. He travels all distance. He makes every effort that all might receive his salvation, that all may experience his grace, that all might eat at his table.

The supply at his table will not adversely affect us. All who feast there enjoy eternal dreams.

LAND OF HERITAGE

The history of Sudan is rich and varied. In fact, the Old Testament word "Cush" and the New Testament word "Ethiopia" refer to Sudan. As early as 580 A.D., there was a Christian presence here and Christian kingdoms ruled the upper river valley until about the 13th century. Things have changed.

Hubert is a man with a heritage. His great-great-great-great-grandfather is a man revered in northern Sudan. This ancestor was the man who preached and established Islam in the north. A large dome sits over his grave and people come from all directions to pray at this shrine, hoping for blessing and invoked favor. This man was instrumental in the now pervasive extent of Islam.

Hubert walks a different path. He is now a follower of the Servant King and has a burden for these lost ones whose fore-fathers walked in the light centuries ago. Hubert deals with the knowledge of his ancestors' corrupting influence in a creative way. He goes to the tomb with the gilded dome and sits outside it. When supplicants begin to arrive, he engages them in conversation. When they ask who he is, he tells them he is a direct descendent of the man they are coming to venerate. This gives him instant respect. Hubert then proceeds to witness to the only true one worthy of worship. He is redeeming his heritage.

I thank God for our Christian heritage in the West but it is crumbling. The disease is more advanced in Europe, but even America is showing tell tale signs of inner decay and moral decline. Sudan, too, was a center for light and truth at one time but it is now overwhelmed with darkness. If the Lord should tarry, but we pray he doesn't, will our homeland one day be totally ignorant of the Truth?

You might think it could never happen. I tell you it already has. It happened here. A godly heritage was abandoned and now we are engaged in a desperate battle to redeem what was lost. We must be diligent and faithful. We cannot rest on our laurels. Whether here in Sudan or in the West with its deceiving comforts, we are swimming upstream against the current and to cease to struggle is to be swept away.

May the Lord bless and encourage you. May you be secure in his heritage. May you be ever seeking to increase his family.

LAND OF SEARCHING

A few weeks ago a plane full of Sudanese officials crashed in the southeast. A dust storm was swirling, eliminating visibility and making it impossible for the pilot to judge wind direction. The pilot, unknowingly, landed with the wind, bounced off the runway, crashed through a fence and splashed into a river. More than 20 people on board died including the vice president. Some bodies were recovered from the crash; others were trapped beneath the waters. A frantic search began – a race between rescuers, the river's current and crocodiles.

Other searches, ones of even more importance, continue.

Sally began searching a year ago. She quietly obtained a Bible from a book exhibition held here in the capital. She began reading it carefully. Just this week she happened to sit down on the bus next to a Christian who happened to be reading a book about the Bible. She could not contain her curiosity and leaned over the shoulder of her neighbor, reading every page. When the lady stood to leave the bus, Sally too disembarked. She followed the woman and said, "That is very interesting. Can you tell me more about the God of the Bible?"

That question led to a long, powerful conversation. After the conversation, Sally took that little, but immense, step of faith and joined the family. Her search has ended. Her eternal future is just beginning.

Please pray for Sudan.

Please pray for similar countries.

Please pray for the multitudes that are searching.

Please pray for more divinely orchestrated bus seat assignments.

Please pray for Sally. She is married with children and knows her husband is going to be furious. May her quiet grace, may the testimony of her changed life, may the love of the Spirit in her, all compel him to embark on a search mission himself – a search with as joyful a result as that of his wife.

May we be living signposts for those stumbling towards truth. Whether in a bus or a McDonalds booth, whether in the market or in the stands of a high school football game, whether in the shadow of the minaret or in the haze of a materialistic society, may we too take the time to point weary searchers to the subject of their desire, our wonderful Savior.

LAND OF SUPPLY

I have written previously about a couple here in Sudan who are believers from an Islamic background. They suffer continually for it. They are secret believers of the not-so-secret kind. They don't tell everybody they have come to faith but they are not shy about witnessing of the Faithful One either.

Some weeks ago Arnie's co-worker stole a gun and blamed it on him. This man had been in Arnie's home numerous times and had even seen the Jesus film there. Arnie was charged with the theft and told he had to come up with an incredible sum of money within a week. It totaled much more than a year's salary. A senior officer added an additional amount to the charge just to make sure it would be impossible for Arnie to come up with the sum. If he failed to do so, a sure thing by their estimation, he would receive a three-year jail sentence.

Arnie and his wife exist at poverty level. For them to raise the money would be like us having to raise around $100,000 cash in a week, with no loans possible and precious few friends. It seemed an impossible situation. But in Sudan the impossible seems to crop up rather often.

Fortunately for Arnie he knew the truth of God, if not the song, "Nothing is too difficult for Thee...." From here, there and everywhere, the funds trickled, streamed, poured and flooded in. In less than a week, he presented himself to the judge and, in the presence of his astounded accusers, laid a staggering amount of money on the table. His prison term was cancelled. There were tears of rejoicing in his home, and scowls and averted looks from his would-be jailers.

The Lord really does supply all our needs. Sometimes we convince ourselves that wants are needs and we get our feelings hurt. But our good Father always knows the difference. In his providence he takes us through just as the song "God Leads Us Along" by George A. Wood says:

> *"Some through the water, some through the flood,*
> *Some through the fire, but all through the Blood;*
> *Some through great sorrow but God gives a song,*
> *In the night season and all the day long."*

LAND OF PARDON
Here in Sudan there is a large prison on the banks of a river. This prison is for those who have committed the worst crimes, those sentenced to death or long imprisonment. But inside is a small growing Christian fellowship.

A murderer condemned to die found his peace with the Lord in this Christian group. As the time drew near for his execution, he grew in faith and trust and faced it calmly. The small group of believers gathered around him. He handed them some money he had saved and said, "Here. I will not need this anymore. You use it for the group."

They all gathered around him and prayed. "You are not going to die!" they told him.

As soon as they finished praying, the guards slapped handcuffs on him and led him away to be hanged. As he stood on the platform, moments away from eternity, a phone call came through. A second reprieve had been granted; he had been given another chance to live.

He walked back into the prison courtyard to the delight of his friends. They began to shout, "HALLELUJAH, HALLELUJAH!" Even the Muslim prisoners, caught up in the joy of the moment, joined in and shouted "Hallelujah," too! This pardon has been a tremendous encouragement to this plucky group.

Millions of others are more condemned in the eyes of a holy God. Millions are steadily walking towards the hangman's noose, sent there by the guilt of sin. The tragedy in Sudan is the deception – a false teaching, a false book, a false hope. People are stumbling towards death and are not even aware of it. That's the bad news.

The good news is Jesus is not without a witness. Small groups, like the one mentioned above – courageous individuals, faithful ones and twos, are carrying the light. They are lifting high the flame. Sudan, unlike many Middle Eastern nations, has a strong Christian minority. They are beginning to grasp the weight of their responsibility. They are beginning to gather in spirit around their Muslim colleagues, friends and neighbors to say: "You don't need to die! There is a hope! There is a way! There is a redemptive plan!"

Please continue to pray for Sudan. Please pray for the millions stumbling toward spiritual death. Please pray for the few who know the rules of pardon. Please pray that they will make him known.

LAND OF TEAMWORK

Undoubtedly, you've heard of a one-man band but have you ever seen a one-man choir? I was speaking at an Eritrean church this morning and to my amazement saw my first one of this rare species. Not only was this solitary figure the whole choir, complete with scarlet robe, he was also the entire instrument section. When the choir was announced, he set his keyboard on autopilot and strode to the pulpit. The keyboard spit out the same one-tone note in endless repetition and our one-voice choir wailed forth.

One song was surprising enough. By the fourth I was astonished. Between each rendition, he would glide to the keyboard, select a different rhythm, which numbingly repeated itself, and he would burst forth in song. It is tough going solo.

The other day we were driving up a steep hill in a pickup truck when we passed a short, heavy-set lady laboring with a pile of vegetables strapped to her back. Our back seat was full but we offered her a ride in the bed of the pickup. The lady threw her load into the truck and struggled valiantly to climb aboard. The truck is quite high off the ground and being stopped on an incline made it higher. The lady's own weight conspired with gravity to resist her efforts. She finally lunged forward, landing on her face. She made it halfway in, but her arms were pinned beneath her. I looked in the rearview mirror to see her legs in the air kicking furiously. It is tough to do it alone.

We thank God for the way he is working here in Sudan. He is forming a team to work together. We, American, Sudanese, English, Eritrean, German, Nigerian, Swedish, Ethiopian, Austrian and Finnish, are not officially organized but are united in spirit with a common goal. By October we hope to have another team member from Malawi. It is futile and dangerous to step out alone. You quickly end up on your face with legs kicking aimlessly in the air. It is so much better to work as a body.

We want to say thanks to you, our fellow team members, who connect us vitally to the Throne room from where the power flows. We know, and we trust you know, your prayers are the backbone of any endeavor on this side. We would be helpless without you. Please continue to pray with us that the Lord will indeed "raise up laborers for the harvest field." Please pray that we will have and maintain a servant's attitude. Some people enjoy the attention of being a one-voice choir but we certainly don't want it to be that way. You might get to pick all the songs but you sure end up looking ridiculous.

LAND OF CONSTITUTION
While it is true that the food and water here in Sudan affect you,

that is not the constitution to which I refer. In a facade proclaiming change, the powers that be have drafted a new constitution that claims religious freedom. Everyone supposedly can worship as they please. Has anyone told that to Mary?

Mary is a Muslim who recently started to follow the Master. Her family is furious and is taking her to court. She is being tried for apostasy. If convicted, she will face death by stoning or will merely be hung.

Two days ago, on the eve of the trial, we sat with her in a secluded compound. Dressed modestly with head covered and bowed, she listened carefully as we shared scripture with her. We had a moving time of singing, prayer and mutual encouragement. She actually encouraged us more than we encouraged her. To see a young girl, totally alone in the natural, face her raging storm with peace was moving. We gave her some Arabic New Testaments and literature that she is planning to give to her family. The trial is now underway and she desperately needs your prayers.

The question could be asked, "Who REALLY is on trial?" Is it brave Mary? Or is it a constitution that declares freedom and then rewards by stoning? In the twisted world of politics and false belief, it is a comfort to remember the Faithful One, the true Judge, sees and understands all.

Lest we be too hasty to condemn others, let us remember our hidden exploits will be revealed before his judgment seat. He sees what we do behind closed doors. He notes what we accomplish with our respective talents. He observes how we respond to his commands. We quickly and rightly embrace him as Savior. But let's not forget that he is Judge. When we stand before him, we will be open to his gaze, exposed and naked.

Speaking of being naked, Mary had a dream in which Jesus appeared to her. He kindly told her to put on her new clothes. She looked down and realized she was covered in filthy rags. "I don't have any new clothes," she said. Jesus again said, "Put on your new clothes!" Then she understood him to mean the clothes of his righteousness, her banquet robe.

It is not yet known what Mary's temporal fate will be. She

may be delivered; she may be killed. We do know we have not seen the last of Mary. Whether here below or in heavenly courts above, we will surely meet again.

LAND OF CHANGE

"Can a leopard change his spots?" The Old Testament writer implies doubt and perhaps he is correct in his reference to physical traits. Can the old become new? Can this sinful flesh become a new creation? I think a dirty, mean, double-crossing, vengeful, angry apostle named Paul would certainly say, "Yes."

A man lives here in Sudan named Freddie. His real name derives from the title given to holy men. They are the ones who write out Koranic spells and charms which are sealed in leather pouches and worn on the arm, around the neck or even on beasts of burden as protection against jinn (spirits). They often also write out curses, which can be buried in the yard of those on whom you wish evil. Freddie is a serious Muslim, devout in all he does.

Two years ago, Freddie came to Christ. As it was for Paul, his zealousness was also purified and redirected. Instead of remaining a devout Muslim, he became serious about Christianity and the Christ. He began to hold meetings in his house and persuaded some of his family to pledge their allegiance to the King. A small fellowship grew.

Ten days ago the security police arrived at Freddie's house. A disgruntled family member had reported the group to the authorities. They pulled Freddie aside and said, "Why have you stopped attending the mosque?"

Freddie replied, "That was two years ago and you just now noticed? If you check up on everybody who does not go to the mosque, you have a lot of work to do!"

Needless to say this did not make the security police happy and Freddie was hauled off to prison. He is being tried for apostasy and if convicted the penalty is death by stoning. Pray for Freddie and his family. He has a young wife and three children. They need us to lift them up. I want to affirm to you, however, that Freddie does not stand alone. Many like him once served a different master but now wholeheartedly follow the Lord. Courageous men and women are following the Savior and paying a tremendous price. By their lives and testimony, they echo the affirmation of Martin Luther, "Here I stand, I cannot, I will not recant."

Let us pray for them even as they challenge us. May we not be ashamed of the gospel in our minor times of testing, while others stand firm against tremendous odds.

LAND OF ONE OF THOSE DAYS

It has been warm in Sudan recently. The other day it was 109 degrees in the house. Yesterday was hot as usual with some minor complications. First, there was no electricity. This is not unusual because we only have electricity every other day and usually for half of the day. We had a water tank made and put on the roof but due to several electricity-less days, the tank was empty by 7 a.m. Then the sewer pipe broke and the septic tank began to rear its ugly head.

A knock on the door of the courtyard brought a needed interruption. A man passing on the street had noticed a bees' nest in some shrubs on our outside wall. He asked if he could collect the honey and I agreed. He donned a plastic bag to cover his head and disappeared into the bushes. I returned to the house, only to hear a crackling noise behind me. I turned and was welcomed by a wall of flame. The man had ingeniously decided to smoke the bees out that day with 110-degree temperature, dry bushes and a dry steady wind. You do the math!

Before we knew it our courtyard was on fire and our bushes raptured. We used our last jug of drinking water in a valiant, but vain, effort to quench the flames. Amazingly, a neighbor called the fire department and even more astonishingly, they quickly arrived and doused the smoking mass with water. The fire had reached high enough to melt our telephone wire. It also scorched one kitty cat and a mattress as well as the bathroom wall and roof. So, now we have no electricity, no water, no sewage system and no telephone. I guess that is one way to cut down on the utility bill!

Yesterday was our first day at home after two years of language study. I think I better go back to Arabic!

LAND OF SELECTIVE DISTURBANCE

Last week was encouraging. We had the privilege of attending two celebration ceremonies. The first one involved the young girl Mary about whom I have written. Mary was to be tried for apostasy. The probable result would have been death by stoning. The day before the trial we sat with her and prayed, sang and shared scripture.

Three days later we sat with her again. In a mysterious turn around, the family had dropped all charges against her. Her face was aglow as she told us. For three days she had not had one problem from her antagonists. She had even taken her younger sisters to a church service without repercussion. We marveled together at the goodness of God.

Later in the week we attended another celebration. I have shared the testimony of some secret believers. This man who works for security was framed by one of his co-workers who found out about his faith. Our friend was given a limited time to raise an incredible amount of money as a fine or face several years in prison. The Lord miraculously provided, and as we sat together to celebrate last week, tears still flowed as we wondered at the goodness of God.

Another Muslim convert, about whom we have written, faces no celebration gathering. He is still locked up in prison accused of crimes against the state. He allegedly made a bomb. The kicker is, he was turned in by another Muslim convert, one with whom we have had contact during the last year and a half. In court the accuser denied his Christian background and quoted liberally from the Koran. Fonzy still waits his day of deliverance.

This selective deliverance can sometimes be puzzling. We have no doubt God works through all situations. We are sure his purposes work towards the good. We are confident faith will triumph in trouble. Yet, the reality is that some are delivered from the circumstance and some are brought through it. Even in biblical history, some were rescued while some were hewn asunder. In all cases, the Lord was glorified; some just hurt more than others. Sometimes we sit in a small room and wonder at God's goodness; other times a solitary and lonely soul sits silent in his chains.

Let us not forget the imprisoned saint can lean back against a hard cement wall. He can shift the chains around his wrists, he can close his eyes and lift up his soul, and he, too, can wonder at the goodness of God.

LAND OF FAMILY

Arabs have long been known for their hospitality. In fact, Bedouins have been known to see a stranger walking towards them through the desert sands and say, "Here comes my guest!" The first one to voice such a remark is the one who has the honor of hosting the stranger.

Family ties are the element that keeps society in order. Families are patrilineal and family honor is a premium. It is commendable behavior for a man, no matter what age, to honor his father's advice even if the advice is wrongheaded. Family honor is the driving force behind the veiled apparel of the womenfolk. To dress modestly is to be treated modestly; to be treated modestly leads to behaving modestly; behaving modestly preserves family honor. Some families will kill their own daughter if she brings shame on them because of a loose lifestyle.

With this understanding we realize the tremendous amount of pressure families put on the members when they become followers of Jesus. Beatings, ridicule, shame and anger are all heaped on the one who becomes a Christian. How would you feel if your only son came to you and announced he had become a gay Buddhist child molester? Pardon the graphic terminology but the revulsion you would feel is akin to that of zealous Muslim families when they find one of their own has left the Islamic faith.

Due to this pressure many converts abandon their families or take different outward forms that further alienate them from their own. They change styles of dress and social behavior that have nothing to do with spiritual things. The family that is the one causing the trouble is the one who feels rejected.

Please pray with us for families here in Sudan. There are some beautiful examples and some tragic ones. One couple we know, "The Dreamers," have incredible ministry together. They pray together in the middle of the night. They go on trips to witness and pass out Bibles. They are amazing! Others have been rejected by family and suffer emotional loss. It is crippling because of the importance of family in this society. Please pray whole households will come to Christ together. They can offer each other so much strength.

Speaking of family, we again thank you, our backbone, for sending and keeping us here. We thank you for holding us up to our Father and Lord. It is by your love we continue.

LAND ON THE MOVE

The country of Sudan is a continual puzzle. The government is a strictly Islamic one and has plans to wipe out Christianity by the year 2000. The powers-that-be see this country as a center for Islamic revolution.

Certain areas are undergoing ethnic cleansing, the sole crime being Christian faith. Muslim converts are imprisoned and sometimes killed. Human rights authorities tell us abuses abound. In fact, more Christians are martyred for their faith in Sudan than in any other country. The country is a haven for militant terrorists. Yet there is a staggering amount of religious freedom. Things possible here are inconceivable in most Islamic countries. The proposed constitution allows Sudanese to believe what they want AND to preach that belief to others.

Some are taking advantage of this paradoxical situation. A church here in town has a growing burden for Muslims. They show gospel films several nights a week on a large screen above the church wall. The church sits adjacent to a market and the whole street, for more than 100 yards, is so tightly packed you can't pass through. On Friday mornings they set up an area in the market and blatantly preach Jesus to the interested throng.

A few weeks ago they miraculously got permission to hold a Jesus March. About 100 people gathered at the church for prayer and then set off. They walked through the main streets of downtown singing and passing out Bibles and tracts. Security had even provided a full riot police escort complete with helmets and shields. The people stopped at main intersections and markets and with a revved up microphone gave a clear gospel witness to the listening Muslim crowds. The police escort had the privilege of hearing the gospel over and over that day! Despite the 115-degree temperature people walked several kilometers and exhausted the supply of books and Bibles. If you walked in the opposite direction of the march, your eyes beheld a beautiful sight: hundreds of Muslims, soldiers, men, women and children bent over Bibles and tracts: some in groups, while others reflected alone. Some in flowing white robes, others in traditional dress. All intently reading what had been handed out.

We often shake our heads in wonder. Most people think the government is trying to put on a good face due to pressure from the West. There is this paradoxical freedom in the capital, yet outside the city where travel is restricted we find unbelievable tyranny. "We must work while it is day." No opportunity lasts forever, so let us seize the moment.

LAND OF BOOKS

Our two years of formal Arabic study came to a close last month. We had a nice graduation and received our certificates both from the university and from the private institute we attended. In celebration we lined up a tutor to start teaching us next week! Arabic is a tough language and we need to stay at it, both in conversation and book study.

By th wy, dd y knw tht rbc s wrttn wtht ny vwls? Ths mks t dffclt t rd, dsnt t? Nt nly r thr n vwls, thr r ls mny strng snds nd prnctn s chllgng!

I just thought you might like to try reading without any vowels. If the above lines did not make sense, the translation is: "By the way, did you know that Arabic is written without any vowels? This makes it difficult to read, doesn't it? Not only are there no vowels, there are also many strange sounds, and pronunciation is challenging!"

The Bible usually has the vowel markings included but journals, newspapers and books usually omit them. Speaking of books, there seems to be a dearth of highly recommended ones on the market. A team of Sudanese recently went to the Western part of the country to hold book exhibitions and sell Bibles and other such literature. The West is 99 percent Islamic and has been traditionally closed to the gospel. They arrived in one large town and set up their tables in the market, expecting to stay for 10 days or so. At the end of the first day, however, they had to modify their plans. EVERY SINGLE BOOK HAD BEEN SOLD. Sheikhs, men, women, youth, all bought books as fast as they could. One old man opened to the Sermon on the Mount and exclaimed, "This is beautiful. Why have our Islamic leaders been keeping this from us?"

Not everyone was happy. One Islamic cleric stormed into the office of the general who was chief of security, dragging some team members with him. He demanded their immediate arrest. The general, himself a Muslim, calmly asked if they were giving the books away or selling them. "They are selling them!" came the startled reply.

The general shrugged and said, "This is a free country. Let them sell!"

The cleric was furious. "This is a Muslim state! We are not under your authority! We follow Allah and not the government!"

The general leaned suddenly forward over his desk and beckoned with his finger, "Come here and say that!"

Our fuming friend chose rather to quickly scurry out the door.

It continually amazes us how the Lord works. He opens doors no man can shut. This is just one story of a multitude of literature that goes out in this land. We carry tracts and New Testaments in our car, and whenever we give someone a lift, we pass them out. I have never once had one refused.

Please pray for all these Muslim people who are reading gospel literature.

Please pray the Spirit will stir them and bring them face to face with the writer of the Book of Life!

LAND OF LEAVING

Sometimes you have to leave a place to get there. Last month was a busy one as we traveled in five different countries. The main purpose was to teach in one of our schools; the difficulty was getting there. Sudan does not have flights directly to some of her neighbors because of war and poor international relations. To get directly east we fly hundreds of miles north and then south again.

After teaching for several weeks in Eritrea, the border with Ethiopia was closed due to fighting. We were booked on Ethiopian Airways to Addis Ababa but the Ethiopian airline discontinued their flights. We were told we would have to purchase an Egyptian Airways' ticket in order to get to our meetings in Addis. We would board the plane in Asmara and fly down to Addis. That sounds straightforward except for the tiny detail that we would not be allowed to get off the plane. Even though Addis was our destination, in order to protect Ethiopian Airways' landing rights, we would have to stay on board and fly "a million miles" to Cairo. We would have to pay for our own hotel in Cairo, fly back to Asmara (our starting point) and then fly down to Addis. We would have to leave Addis in order to arrive there to take this flight.

We often do not appreciate something until we have lost it. As soon as we leave a place, our selective memory kicks in and we begin to forgive its difficulties. If you ask me now about my years at boarding school, I will sing its praise. But if you ask my parents, they will tell you my nightly prayer request always concerned correspondence courses. This principle is not restricted to migration and physical geography. We only own what we give away. We only rule what we have surrendered. We only retain what we release.

So often we are locked into the deceptions of this world, as we clutch, hoard and scheme for self-advancement, only to see those elusive desires recede. What a revelation it is to see joy in giving, freedom in surrender and liberty in service. We tend to think in terms of what is lost and fail to see how much we have to gain by losing. How quickly we can arrive by leaving.

LAND OF TROUBLE

A bare 4 x 4 foot cell. Tightly bound chains. Throbbing limbs. An open sewage hole. No food or water for three days. 120 degrees. Constant beatings. No sleep. No rest. No escape. For three days Abraham endured these conditions. He has been through two weeks of hell. Security first picked him up a few weeks ago. "Why do you associate with foreigners? What can you tell us about them?" Huge amounts of money were placed before him. "If you work for us, we will give you all this money. We will buy you a new house. We will send your children to the best schools."

Abraham quietly refused and said, "No, thank you, I am quite happy the way I live now." More beatings, more torture, more suffering. Security dropped him off at home. He could barely walk. He struggled to speak. "Think it over for a month," they said. "We will be back."

Two days later, they arrived in the middle of the night and dragged Abraham back to his little cell. More beatings, more threats, more torture and more abuse followed. His family had no idea where he was. Several days later he was dumped back home. His body was battered; his spirit was heavy. He looked so terrible his wife and two small children were afraid of him. They thought he had lost his mind. "If you tell anyone what has happened," he was warned, "we will come and kill your children." They are coming after his wife next. The family knows this and they are accepting it with peace.

Abraham painfully made his way to the doctor. In the waiting room he began to tell people about Jesus. His wife elbowed him in the side, saying, "Shut up! That is why we are in this trouble."

Some things cannot be contained. Some fires rage in the bones that no trouble can extinguish. They understand Jesus' promise: "In this world you will have trouble, but fear not, I have overcome the world." Some people wade deeply into the promises of Jesus, but most of us paddle around their shores.

All of us have concerns. Jesus takes our struggles seriously. On the scales of your own personal injustices and tragedies, I ask you to add the counterbalance of those of Abraham and his wife. Though real, our troubles are relative. Many others stand on the promises of God in spite of great difficulties. In the midst of our scratches, let us stand with them in their time of deep wounds. On Wednesday, June 24, we are asking everyone we know to stand with Abraham and his family in their time of testing. Would you consider joining us? Could you set aside a few hours to intercede for them. Friends in Sudan, Germany and Sweden have already pledged to stand with us. Will you do so as well?

LAND OF SNOWFLAKES

I returned yesterday from a trip to the eastern part of Sudan. Ten years ago this was a totally Islamic area. Now as a result of war, thousands of refugees have fled here from the South. Many of these dear folks are Christians. Small fellowships have started to spring up in every village of the East and North. God surely moves in mysterious ways.

A few days ago we were in one of these fellowships. They had constructed a mud church, equipped with a mud roof, pulpit and pews. The temperature outside was above 110 degrees and inside it felt almost double because of a full house and lack of ventilation. Five minutes into the service, you could see that everyone's clothes had changed color as a result of flowing sweat. A darling little boy sat in rapt attention in front of me with perspiration falling in numerous tributaries down his solemn face.

When it was time for the message, one of our group stood to address the gathered throng. His name is Fermo, a pastor from southern Sudan. Sweat cascaded down his dark features and I started to wonder if he had sprung a leak. The sweat was running in his eyes and he was having trouble reading his text. I remembered a bit of tissue I had in my pocket and I placed it on the pulpit for him. He grabbed it gratefully and mopped his brow. In seconds, the tissue was a soggy mess.

Fermo continued to dab at his face with the sodden tissue during the course of his sermon. Unbeknownst to him, the tissue was beginning to disintegrate and cling in little flecks to his face. Fermo is a very dark man and the white specks of tissue stood out as stars of white. The congregation watched in amusement as Fermo's face became increasingly spotted. The polka-dotted preacher continued in blissful ignorance, his snowflaky appearance somehow not quite meshing with his serious message.

How often are our words contradicted by our behavior and appearance, especially those of us in ministry who become adept at saying the right things and even saying them forcefully. I suspect when we loudly proclaim the truth and yet stumble in our personal application of it, we look rather like my dark-skinned friend with a face full of snowflakes. The attention of all of us in that place was fixed on the living painting and not on the words he proclaimed. Please pray that our actions will confirm our message and not detract from it.

LAND OF FREEDOM

What a wonderful thing it is to be free. Nothing underlines that simple truth more than the lack of freedom and its subsequent restoration. After two days in prison, I can testify to that.

I left the house at 5 a.m. with three others for a four-hour trip through the desert to the north. We were carrying 15 cases of Bibles and Christian literature. We planned to stop in a certain town and distribute the Good Book and then drive another six hours on a desert track to a different village and a brand new church.

By 10 a.m., at the last checkpoint before our destination, we were arrested. Thus began the longest two days of my life, filled with eternal interrogation, humiliating treatment, lack of food, hostility and harshness. We were accused of being CIA, we were threatened and we were treated as errant children.

From 10 a.m. until 4:30 a.m. the next morning, the interrogation continued. We attempted to answer truthfully but vaguely. Every inch of our clothing was searched, every bag and box of Bibles were emptied. I will never forget the sound of the cell door slamming shut, the bolt being thrown home and the echoing click of a padlock being snapped in place.

We were allowed two hours of sleep and at 6 a.m. the questioning began again. They finally fed us a light meal of yogurt at 10 and then set us out in the blazing courtyard sun. At noon, they decided to take us back to the capital. Though there was space in the cabs of the two pickups (mine and a government one), we were forced to sit in the bed of the pickups and endure the midday sun on the four-hour ride. Once we arrived in the city, we endured more questioning and rude treatment until 8 at night.

At 8 o'clock the director for security arrived at the compound where we were being held. In a miraculous turn of events, he told us, "The President signed a new constitution yesterday. We now have religious freedom in Sudan. We apologize for the mix up. You are free to go!" He assured us that we could return to the city and distribute the Bibles and he would issue us all the proper documents, informing the security personnel in that place. We walked out of the door wondering at the goodness of God.

I knew Jennifer was in a prayer meeting. I was very tempted to knock on the door and declare, "Rhoda, go tell the group Peter is here!"

The Lord is good and in a few days we will return to the same city and shower love of those who have treated us so badly. We have our freedom. In fact, we never lost it but they continue to be bound.

LAND OF FREEDOM 2

Here is a detailed account of the generic e-mail I sent.

Usually when you travel, you need travel documents and I have usually been careful to get them. This time I didn't, however, for two reasons. The place I was going is not in a troubled area.

Last year I drove there for a visit without incident. On this trip I was taking a lot of Bibles, and if I were caught, it would reflect badly on George, the Greek who gets the documents for me. I was traveling with a fellow Pentecostal from Nigeria, an intern from Southwestern University and a Sudanese brother who knew the way to the villages we wanted to visit in the desert.

We made it safely through all the checkpoints until the last one. There Kennedy (the Sudanese) unwisely mentioned we were with the church. I usually simply say we are going visiting and they often wave us on. As soon as they heard the word "church," we were in trouble. They took us to the army barracks and the questioning began.

After some time, we were led to a lounge filled with security men. The three guys I traveled with were tense and the atmosphere was a little gloomy, so I asked the security guys if I could play ping-pong with them. There was a table there and they agreed. This loosened them up. I lost the first game to an officer and one of them said, "Americans are no good at ping-pong!"

The spirit of Smith (competition) rose up in me and I played that officer next, spanked him and said in Arabic, "The Sudanese are no good at ping-pong!" This made the others laugh but he was not too thrilled.

They then had me take the car to a compound and they searched everything. In Kennedy's bag, they found a pair of green khaki pants like the ones issued to the military. They belonged to his brother and he had forgotten to take them out of his bag. This was a further blow to us and things spiraled downward. They, of course, thought he was with the rebels and I was CIA. They kept asking me, "Where have you hidden the weapons?"

I said, "The only weapon we have is the Word of God."

After more questions, we were taken to the chief of security. By now it was four o'clock in the afternoon and we had not had any food all day. The chief had a bee in his britches and treated us like dirt. We were never beaten, just humiliated. They questioned us continually until 4:30 a.m. They demanded my car keys, which I surrendered grudgingly. I had anticipated the request and had

PART ONE

locked the car with the crook lock and hidden the key between the layers of my shoe. The imperative verb in Arabic "sallim," meaning surrender, is similar to "salim," the imperative of "greet." (The difference is a double L.) When the chief demanded I surrender the keys to a group of security all decked out in white robes and turbans, I turned to them, lifted both hands and in a friendly voice said, "Salaam alaikum!" ("Peace upon you," the traditional greeting.) They looked at me like I was Ronald McDonald.

They let us sleep for over an hour. At 6 a.m., the questioning began again. In my mind I started to think about where the Lord would have us go next. Chad? Mauritania? Eritrea? I was certain this was it for Sudan. In the security compound they spread the Bibles out on the half wall of a simple mosque. Whenever security agents came to pray, we watched with interest as they couldn't contain their curiosity. Almost to a man, they picked up scriptures and started reading. We were questioned from 6 a.m. until noon and then transported through the desert back to the capital.

In the capital we started off in a holding office that opened up to an alleyway. While we were waiting, I saw a young shoeshine boy saunter pass. I asked if I could get my shoes shined. The officer agreed and I slipped the boy a note and whispered in Arabic that he should take it to the nearest white person. I wanted someone to know where we were.

It was a great idea but the boy did not find a white person. He found a worker from the SIM compound who wasn't too bright. The worker came to security and turned in the note. Needless to say, my fat was in the fire. We were immediately hauled out and the questioning heated up.

Meanwhile, the SIM worker realized his mistake and called the SIM director. She contacted Jennifer. Word quickly spread and impromptu prayer meetings cropped up all over the city.

The questioning went on until the chief for all security issues in Sudan arrived. He treated us kindly and said, "Yesterday the president signed the new constitution into law. You have your freedom to do as you like. I apologize for the trouble. Here are all your documents. You are free!"

101

I thanked him and reminded him that security was holding all our Bibles and things in the north. I asked if we could collect them. He said, "No problem, I will deal with it right now. You can go back and give out the Bibles. You can preach to Christians. You can even talk to Muslims. We will not convert," he said with a smile, "but you can preach to us. We need to hear what you are saying." He went on. "Whenever you need to travel, come to me and I will make the arrangements."

Instead of having two hours to pack my bags, I now have an open invitation. Our God is surely something! I am going back on Sunday to see if the security chief is as good as his word. We still aren't sure if he was trying to smooth over a potentially difficult situation or if he is sincere. We will surely call his hand, however. Wouldn't it be ironic to have government permission to do what has been denied for so long? We will proceed carefully but pro-actively. I admit, the flesh in me looks forward to heading back north on Monday we hope, to see these men who imprisoned us and treated us shamefully and are now ORDERED to aid us. Hah! You cannot mess with God.

P.S. I decided I do not like prison but at least it was free!

LAND OF PROCESS

My mother recently sent me an airmail package. It weighed 15 pounds and contained used clothes and a few books. In the States it would have taken about five minutes to clear it through customs. In Sudan it took me four days of work. Along the way I "enjoyed" extensive visits in 18 different offices and four major government ministries. I am now familiar with the Ministry of Trade, the Department of Taxation, the Ministry of Health and the Department of Customs and Immigration. I paid 11 different taxes, including a food tax and an alcohol tax. This last tax was especially ironic since that substance is banned. At the end of my travels, I had a half-inch thick file full of receipts, applications and forms filled out in triplicate. The process was taxing (!) but it was all worth it when I carried the box home in triumph.

Last month we made repeated attempts to get Bibles to a town in the north. Our first trip landed us in jail as you have heard. After a miraculous release we made a second attempt, carrying with us a security officer who was to insure our safe passage. After traveling for four hours through the desert sands, we were again turned back after a six-hour detention. We attempted a third trip this morning but were not able to leave the city. We have an appointment on Monday with the head of security, and if he issues us written permission, we will try our desert trek one more time. We have been in and out of his office numerous times in the last few weeks. At various times we have not been allowed in; at others we could not leave. The process is tedious but we know the end will be rewarding.

We all are in process. On some days my personal failings rise up as a flood and stare me down. At other times the weight of trial and circumstances seem overpowering. The process, the journey is steadily consuming. What redemption is found in being reminded the process is temporary. What a joy to realize the weight, sorrow and trouble we momentarily experience only sweeten the eventual arrival. I am in process; Jesus is changing me. This world is in process; he is redeeming it to himself. With a shout, with trumpet sound, with praise and great glory, the process will be declared complete and we shall be like him. It will be worth it all when we see Jesus!

LAND OF DETERRENCE

Some time ago a man was arrested for stealing. As you know Sharia, Islamic law governs Sudan and the prescribed penalty for that offense is the amputation of an appendage. The judge wanted to make a further impact on the unfortunate offender and demanded the severed hand be tied around his neck and worn as a constant reminder.

In a different vein the lack of electricity here serves as a deterrence to work. The 110-plus degree days are tolerable with the help of a fan; without it, lethargy creeps up like a bandit. At night we have become accustomed to frequent power cuts. Often the most immediate solution is to carry around a laptop until we can find candles by its light. It is not often, except in the military, you can claim to use a $2,500 flashlight.

On a final semi-related note, life insurance is illegal in Sudan. Under the Islamic system things like this, as well as interest charged by the bank, are not allowed. Both would seem to deter investment and long-term planning.

I mention these physical facts only because they remind me of spiritual hurdles. I heard an old World War II bomber pilot quoted as saying "We knew we were over the target when they started firing at us."

In recent weeks we have been very aware that God is moving in this place. At the same time with the victories have come tremendous challenges against what he is doing. The enemy of our souls has unleashed his vile agents against both others and us. From without and within we are confronted with things that could discourage, dismay or deter us.

We are reminded in these challenges that we cannot, that we must not give up. Rather "we set our eyes not on what we see but on what we cannot see. What we see will last only a short time, but what we cannot see will last forever."

LAND OF CONVERSION

Sudan is a diverse land. Its large Christian minority allows us more witnessing opportunities than many other Middle Eastern nations. Unfortunately that door swings both ways. We recently heard of an American working in the partially open embassy who has converted to Islam. Those now seeking asylum for reasons of religious freedom will have to apply through him.

Many Southerners have also converted to Islam. One of those committed a serious crime and was condemned to be hung. While in prison he met a group of Christian prisoners and dedicated his life to Jesus. Though his soul had found peace, his sentence remained and on the appointed day he was led before the warden.

"Before I am hung," he said, "I want it known that I am dying a Christian."

"You can't!" came the astonished reply. "We have already dug your grave in the Muslim cemetery."

"Well, you can bury me where you want," our friend replied, "but someday soon the trumpet will sound, the Lord will descend from heaven with a shout and one of those graves in the Muslim cemetery is going to burst open. I will rise to meet my Savior in the air!"

We sometimes forget the imminent return of our Lord. Lately the Lord has been reminding me that he is surely coming. Every Christian since Antioch has lived in that hope and expectation. We too must live in it and long for it. "This gospel of the kingdom will be preached in the whole world as a testimony to all nations, and then the end will come" (Matthew 24:14). Amen. Maranatha! Come, Lord Jesus.

LAND OF HOLLOW PRAYER

Every morning we are serenaded by what seems to be disenfranchised grinding machines.

Five times a day, with stunning variety, the hundreds of minarets around this city beckon their faithful to prayer. Some Imams relish their 30 seconds of power and drag out their utterance to misery. Others seem embarrassed and rush through the prayer call like a taxi driver in Cairo. Our neighborhood squawker has serious issues with phlegm. Driving home at sunset exposes you to numerous upturned bottoms, the exclamation points for both piety and hypocrisy.

It is not their hollow prayer I am concerned about today. At 5:20 this morning I got up to meet with some men for prayer. I rushed from there to a team prayer meeting at 8:00. From that prayer I ran to the Bible school chapel. From the chapel I talked briefly with a few students and staff, and prayed with a visitor in my office. Before I could blink thrice, it was 1:30 p.m. My day had been filled with prayer and I was the worse for it.

Perhaps this letter will only be relevant to a few, perhaps not. My life is leading people in prayer, study and scripture knowledge, and in the dissemination of the claims of Christ. This is a wonderful privilege and I would not trade it even for Michael Jordan's vertical, Veggie Tales' popularity or President George W. Bush's influence. In the process of a life that is centered in leading people to Jesus, it is terribly easy to lose sight of the Savior himself.

It hit me with force today: I have been helping people all day enter his presence, without plunging in myself. I feel like a scalper hawking tickets outside a World Series game. A head full of knowledge being used to sell people my wares, but far from the pulsating crowd of worshippers. I want to be a front row worshipper. I want to continue to lead others to Jesus, but not at the expense of my soul. This can obviously be a both/and rather than an either/or proposition. I ask your prayer even as I pray for you. Let us be people who are personally and constantly familiar with God's presence. From there, let us rock our worlds.

LAND OF REALLY BIG GUYS

Last week I took Luke to watch his first basketball game. A touring team from the West was in Sudan to play local club teams. We found our way to a second row seat and plunked ourselves down. Within moments, perhaps the most famous current Sudanese of all strolled in and interminably eased himself into the chair next to us.

I say interminably because Manut Bol is over 7 feet 6 inches tall and it took about three minutes for him to move from a standing to a sitting position. Manut is best known for being the walking tree that used to sit the bench for several NBA teams. Manut chatted the whole game, and when Luke and I left at halftime, I said, "Luke, say goodbye to Manut!" Luke refused and shoveled his hands in his armpits, singularly unimpressed with the giant before him. Manut stretched out his racquet of a hand and tickled Luke on the belly.

A friend I will call Abel found himself in prison for fraud. He had written a large check on rubber and the resulting rebound landed him in the clink. He was a judge and an imam, a man pretty impressed with himself despite his obvious deficiency in integrity. In prison he encountered a believer who'd been incarcerated for his faith in Christ. Abel determined it was his moral duty to restore his fallen inmate to Islam and set out aggressively to do so. Things did not work out as planned however, as Jesus in the imprisoned believer began to shine out on Abel.

One night, the believer (we'll call him Fred) stood up to pray. Abel was impressed at his simple sincerity. When Fred lay down to sleep, Abel suddenly and violently nudged him. "Fred, they are calling me to pray!"

"Who is calling you to pray," Fred asked.

"Those really big guys along the wall," exclaimed Abel.

Stretching around the room were men who reached from the floor to the 10-foot ceiling. They had shimmering, non-distinct faces. Fred could not see them, so he shrugged, rolled over and said, "Well then, go pray!"

"But I do not know what to pray," said Abel nervously.

Fred replied, "Just praise Jesus and tell Him that you love Him."

Abel began to simply pour out his heart to the Lord, and Jesus responded by rushing in with saving faith. Today, Abel has been released from prison and is a member of our local body. He is growing in faith despite great opposition. He has met the biggest guy of all and has been decidedly impressed. Trusting that today Jesus breaks through the dream world we call life and looms large upon you.

LAND OF EDUCATION

I believe there is great money to make in the proofreading business. Jennifer and I always get a chuckle from reading translated menus, street signs, and brochures.

I am currently being slowly deafened by a giant and malcontent tsetse fly that attempts to pass itself off as a Russian propeller plane. As I disembarked this noisy pest on the outward leg of my journey, I was greeted by the hand-lettered announcement over the rear door, "EXSIT." I deduced it must be time to stand.

As I walked through this bustling town in Darfur, I saw signs that said "SMILEY CLICK" (a photography studio), "FREEZERS

AND AIR-CONDITIONAL" (inferring I suppose that cool air was optional), and a warning against "INFECTICUS SUBSTANCES" (probably smuggled directly from the original Latin). Though I love the variety of error in translation, not all education is as harmless.

This Western area of Sudan is plagued by the slave trade. Some time ago, school children brought home a sanctioned announcement regarding a school outing. They were told to prepare for a two-day field trip. Uncertain parents checked with the school administration and were assured that all was in order. On the departure day when the children arrived at school to board the bus, internal alarms started clanging, for there were no Muslim children aboard. The bus was then driven through the desert to a neighboring country where the children were held in prison-like conditions and forced to memorize the Koran. This happened several years ago and anguished parents have spent agonized days searching for their lost little ones.

This event is painful enough for me to experience vicariously as I think about how I would feel if my two precious sons were abducted and brainwashed – let alone to experience the dreadful reality. As I sat in the crowded airport waiting for my dysfunctional tsetse fly to buzz in and fetch me, I begin to muse about other lost little ones. The population of the area I visited now approaches six million and we only know about one or two indigenous believers. Another anxious eternal Father has spent years and tears longing for His lost ones.

Friends, your prayers are priceless; they are lifelines. Yet we are desperately short of searchers. Won't you come help us? We have a lot of finding to do and we need your eyes and your hands – in complement to your knees.

LAND OF BAD PROGRAMMING
A friend of mine who is active in outreach to Muslims was discouraged last week. Instead of attending the weekly prayer meeting he decided to stay home and watch TV. He happened upon a local Sudanese talk show, which is hosted by a renowned Islamic

sheikh. The sheikh receives telephone calls and pontificates grandly in response.

"Yes, caller number one," said the Sheikh.

"Is it wrong for me to read the New Testament?"

"Yes, caller number two," said the sheikh.

"My wife just converted to Christianity after 20 years of marriage, what do I do?"

"Yes, caller number three," said the sheikh.

"Every time I try to pray, I see a vision of a bejeweled cross. What does that mean?"

This particular program is broadcast by satellite across the Middle East and the Sheikh stumbled and bumbled for answers, vainly trying to cover his anger. It was evident to every viewer – and encouraging to my disheartened friend – that God is mightily moving in this land, stirring the hearts of Muslims toward himself. After hearing these testimonies, we are thinking of adding a "call-in" phase to our ministry. Telephones lend a measure of privacy, and we think we could send some humdinger questions sizzling towards our now nervous Sheikh!

It matters not whether the context is Sudan or North Dakota for the reality is that this world cannot satisfy the deepest longings of our hearts. Neither Islam nor iced tea can quench our spiritual thirst. Therefore people all over this globe are looking for truth and fulfillment. I encourage you not to despair, but to keep your antennas up and notice the veiled signs that indicate a people desperate for ultimate meaning. Their hunger screams out at us – we only need adjust our hearing aids.

LAND OF WASTE

My travels last month included a trip to Fez, Morocco. The old city section of Fez alone houses over 450,000 citizens, virtually all of which are Muslim. With friends I donned my tourist hat and toured the twisting alleyways and crowded city markets. We gazed and gawked with the best of them as we tramped by tanneries, carpet warehouses, and hidden antique stores that housed dusty treasures.

As we walked through the ancient streets, I could not help but think of the tremendous waste. For hundreds of years and multiple generations, the inhabitants of Fez have been poured into hell like so much discarded cabbage. For over a thousand years, almost every single inhabitant of this city has been discarded for eternity. We would balk at emptying our retirement account to use as kindling. Yet do we even blink at the wasted humanity that steadily marches to damnation?

It is easier not to think about it. It is easier not to let the realities of tragedy affect our emotions. It is easier to insulate ourselves in our own merry and less complicated world. It is easier not to grapple with cities and nations that generation after generation are being cavalierly tossed into the dumpster of Satan.

May we become determined that the lives we live not be wasted. May we not compound the problem by frittering away our lives in frivolous and self-centered living. I love my sons desperately. I want to invest in them. But do I exist only to raise them so that they may raise their sons who will in turn raise my great grandchildren? What a waste if the sum total of my existence is just to survive and propagate my own bloodline.

There is so much more: There are millions of other sheep that have not yet heard the Shepherd's call. Let us not waste any opportunity we have to avail to them an invitation – an invitation to Jesus and an eternity secure.

LAND OF GROVEL

Three days ago I headed north into the desert with a Muslim friend. Ismail belongs to a Sufi order of Muslim mystics. For some time he has been asking me to visit his sheikh. "This man can tell the future. He can tell you all about your life. He is wonderful! You must come and meet him," he said. I agreed to go on the condition that we wanted equal time to share with this mystic legend.

It was ebony dark by the time we arrived in this remote desert village. We had bumped through noiseless sands and moon-like landscape and arrived a sand snake's wiggle from the edge of nowhere. We stepped out of my car and into the third century (the third century before Christ!).

The sheikh is an old, semi-lucid aesthetic, with a charming sense of humor. He rules like a king, setting up his throne by perching on a simple reed mat in the middle of a barren stretch of pebbles. His followers gather round him with faces pressed toward the earth, not daring to lift their eyes and scurrying to obey his every order.

A simple lantern was placed in our midst, illuminating the first few rings of prostrate disciples, with outer rings receding in the darkness. People from all over Sudan were present: some asking for blessing, others for guidance. Prayers were muttered, charms chanted, gifts were offered (one of which was a guinea sack of onions which was deposited in my truck), with a lot of groveling serving as garnishing in between. When his attention was turned to us, I asked him simply if men might have assurance of eternity with God after death. This wizened old man pontificated and the group of devoted around him mumbled their assent and approval to his circular logic.

As the sheikh continued to drizzle drivel, it became more apparent that he was a simple old man without a clear grasp of either the Qur'an or the Hadiith. A colleague with me (a Sudanese saved out of Islam) asked directly – and unwisely – if Mohammed knew for sure that he was going to Paradise. The crowd erupted into shouts, and a shadowy figure raced out of the darkness and slammed the lantern. The hair on the back of my neck stood at attention. The sheikh answered angrily and our pleasant conversation turned into a one-sided shouting match. We were dismissed from his court, escorted out of the village, pointed in the general direction of home and left to find our own way through the desert.

Many of the Sheikhs of this world whether they rule over a little band of Muslim followers, a Fortune 500 company, or a household of two toddlers and an alcoholic husband will not be reached by sterling apologetics or threatening questions. Many will only be reached through consistent love expressed through practical relationship complemented by miracles, dreams or a power encounter. May we "always be prepared to give an answer for the hope that we have" (1 Peter 3:15) but may we also know the hope Himself so intimately that we expect and allow Him to act supernaturally whether through us or despite us.

LAND OF THE FRATERNAL

My two little men, Luke and Zack, continue to grow and give us much joy. Their proximity in age to one another causes many to ask if they are twins. But really their physical attributes and personal characteristics could not be more different.

Luke is built like a Lubbock parking meter (no bottom, all head). Zack is more like a London postbox (cylindrical and fire-haired). Luke will probably one day win a Nobel Prize for atomic biochemical fusion dispersion theory (as contained in blue Lego blocks), while Zack is already looking for the next Light Brigade with which he can charge stubbornly into battle. Luke's coloring is Grecian olive and Zack's as a bleached refugee from Dublin. Luke's cranium could house a cannon ball while Zack's looks like it got squeezed in the elevator doors on the way out of the hospital. Yet, because of their differences, they are both desperately loved.

Sudan is also composed of two such dissimilar brothers. Southern Sudan is green; northern Sudan is sand. Southern Sudan is African; northern Sudan is Arabic. Southern Sudan is ravaged; northern Sudan enjoys an eerie calm. Southern Sudan is nominally Christian; northern Sudan holds a passel of pluralist Muslims. Two very different brothers both desperately loved by their eternal Father.

There are current twin concerns for our land – both valid. One is the plight of southern Sudan with the ongoing atrocities by both sides. Thousands have been rushed prematurely to the judgment seat. The second is the anemic slipping of millions of Muslims from the North into the horror of an eternity they are not prepared for. Please continue to pray with us for both concerns. Please pray that we might be wise and brave. Please pray that these two brothers so long at odds will soon be reconciled to each other and to the Father who longs for them.

LAND OF BLOOD-RED EYES

A young woman I will call Nellie is seeing red today. Nellie is a delightful lady of Arab origin. A year ago or so, she professed her faith that Jesus is who He claims to be according to our uncorrupted Scriptures. She has been growing steadily in her faith and her smile is one of peace and joy.

Last week her sister pretended to be interested in the gospel message. After leading Nellie deceitfully into revealing more of what she believed, the sister suddenly sprang up and ran to bring in a different relative. Nellie was frog-marched away and beaten so badly by her flesh brother that she began to bleed out of her eyes. She was rushed to hospital, and since that day we have not seen her again.

When buildings are bombed, friends are beaten and loved ones damaged, it is entirely possible for us to be blinded by the red mist ourselves. I want to challenge you, and include myself in the questioning: What kind of blood covers our eyes? Is it the rage of injustice? Is it fear that leads to the doubting of anyone of Arab visage? Is it the horror of a world gone wrong? Is it even the natural plasma that flows from a real, personal and painful tragedy – a beating akin to Nellie's?

Or is it the blood of the Passover Lamb?

Let us not be surprised when a world gone wrong from inception naturally bears the fruit it has been groomed to produce. May our eyes be covered with the blood of Jesus. He too had literal blood in His eyes. Blood that He had to squint through as He forgave the representative cousins of ours who beat Him so mercilessly. May we also decide to be so bold.

LAND OF POP QUIZZES

In a city south of us, a little girl slipped to her knees to pray.

There is nothing unusual about little girls, nor is there anything uncommon about them praying on their knees. But this little girl happened to be in the middle of a school, in the middle of a lesson, and in the middle of Muslim peers.

Outside the windows of the school, across a dusty field, brave souls had started an evangelistic campaign. They were too far away to hear, and buildings and trees obscured any view. The little girl had no possible physical connection to the activities – none at least that the Spirit needed.

As the girl slipped to her knees, the class and teacher stalled, stuttered and stopped. The little girl began to pray in tongues and in fact fell prostrate on her face immersed in the presence of God.

Though I am not sure the particular infection of the Spirit coursing through her, one thing was evident – it was the contagious variety. Every child in that classroom fell out of their chairs and spontaneously began to worship Jesus. The Spirit glided through the wall to the connected row of classrooms and soon the entire school was on its face, crying out to the Lord in intercession. Ladies in the neighborhood began running out of their houses, tears streaming down their faces, praying, groaning, speaking in languages that they did not know. The principal was so shaken that he shut down the school for three days; he could not believe the witness of his own eyes.

Sometimes school can surprise you. Sometimes God rattles us out of our conventions and norms. Sometimes God's Spirit yearns so fiercely for worshipers that he overflows the banks of his own methods in order to bring His lost ones home. God's preferred method for shaking the nations is to use individuals to love individuals. Therefore His "glory outbursts" should not remove our responsibility. They should stir us once again towards His passion "that none should perish."

And our little "pop quiz" must be this simple question: Does our passion for lost souls remotely resemble the Father's? If not, may I suggest that you slip out of whatever school bench you are comfortably squatted on and spend a few minutes with our brave little sister on your knees.

LAND OF FROGS

When the frantic Pharaoh waved goodbye to his forest of web-footed courtesans, little did he know they would migrate south. Our son Luke has taken the opportunity to use these hoppers to his advantage where Moses left off. Luke will run around the garden and catch these little springers to give as gifts to houseguests. With his little hands clenched and his bright blues sparkling he approaches the unwary and asks, "Would you like a frog?" Most visitors think to themselves, "What a cute little urchin, I will of course play along with his little imaginative scenario." And they say something politely naïve such as, "I would be delighted."

The usual sequence of events is then: 1) Luke places slimy frog in outstretched hand, 2) visitor stretches out a scream and hurls the hopper across the room, 3) Luke howls with his own delight and scurries off to find more amphibian accomplices.

I usually like to play the guitar early in the mornings when I rise to pray, and one day I noticed a somewhat muffled sound emanating from the reluctant strings. I looked down to see one of Luke's unfortunate captured web-foots stuffed between the strings and the base of the guitar, splayed out on his back in resigned eternal discomfort. It is somewhat challenging to strum "Hallelujah" with a dead frog sharing the strings. I had to settle for the little known chorus "Father, FROGive him for he knows not what he does."

We often act like little Lukes before our heavenly Father. We proudly -and sometimes mischievously - present Him with an offering that we have scurried around like mad to apprehend. He gladly receives it, not because it is intrinsically precious and desired, not really because we have worked so hard to catch it, and probably not because it is slimy, but because He loves us and He is incurably patient. Luke's little frog deposits have made me reevaluate my scurrying. I have given pause to ponder and ask myself just what kind of gifts I am want to bring, and with what motive have I placed them in the Father's hand.

LAND OF POWER

Three nights ago we held an all-night prayer meeting to coincide with the Islamic Night of Power. The last 10 days of Ramadan are considered by Muslims to contain extra blessing for the devout, and the Night of Power especially so, as it commemorates the alleged descent of the Qur'an to Mohammed. The following is a testimony of what transpired this week:

Mazhar (a pseudonym) approached a believer and stated emphatically, "I do not want to hear about Mohammed. I do not want to hear about Jesus. I just want to hear the truth." The believer simply replied, "Go home and pray, ask the true God to reveal himself." The man agreed and the next morning returned early with elated visage.

"Last night I had a dream. I dreamt I was in a hospital ward full of wounded men and women. Beds were laid alongside an endless aisle and hosted the cripple, soiled, battered and burdened. All of a sudden, a man in shining white appeared at the end of the room. His face shone and he carried a flaming world on top of a long staff. As he slowly walked by these hospital beds, every suffering and bound captive jumped up absolutely healed. When he stopped at my bed and looked piercingly at me, I could only whimper, 'What must I do?' He told me to come here, and therefore, here I stand."

In a true power encounter, Mazhar lost and submitted his future to King Jesus. G.K. Chesterton observes, "It may be said with rough accuracy that there are three stages in the life of a strong people. First, it is a small power and fights small powers. Then it is a great power and fights great powers. Then it is a great power and fights small powers, but pretends that they are great powers, in order to rekindle the ashes of its ancient emotion and vanity. After that, the next step is to become a small power itself."

Our Christian heritage has left us a great legacy, but I am very much afraid that we are on the cusp of reverting to "small power." The struggle for individual souls is the heart of the matter – it is also the battlefield for the power struggle within our own hearts.

Will the fuel that drives us come from self-love or a love for the lost? The energy source will very much dictate whether or not we finish the race "small" or "great."

LAND OF GIVING

Last week a friend of mine named Joe went to visit his neighbor. The neighbor was not Sudanese but a depressed and inebriated Czechoslovakian. Our drunken comrade pontificated on the evils of organized church and the merits of communism in between large swallows of non-water. In time Joe was able to gently but passionately share Christ with him. Our inebriate sobered up a little bit and desired to present Joe with a gift.

"Jolly" wandered off, only to return with a case of 24 beers. As Joe stuttered his pseudo-thanks, our somewhat alert Marxist tottered off to bring six cans of pork as well. Realizing that pork and beer are taboo in Muslim society, an embarrassed Joe again tried to politely decline. In one last Herculean effort, our valiant friend ambled back with a package of ham. Joe sheepishly made his way home through the neighborhood carrying a case of beer, six tins of pork and a packet of ham, and feeling much like a machine gun-toting, Klan cape-wearing, "Bin Ladin for School Board" lapel pin-sporting Afghani in a New York airport.

This Christmas season I have been challenged again to evaluate what kind of presents I lay at the feet of the nail-adorned Christ-Cross tree. I rush to load the oft-inappropriate gifts of effort, idea, program and plan into the arms of a patient Savior. In his grace, a patient Savior receives what I drunkenly give, waiting all the time for sobriety and the sacred gift of my self, my all, my will.

May I, may you, this Christmas give Christ a gift that he can revel in, one that he can joyfully parade before all men.

LAND OF BOND

One of the things that we do in Sudan is pastor Khartoum Christian Center (KCC). A growing congregation of about 75 people that meets on Friday morning. Our church is a mixture of southern

Sudanese, expatriates and Muslim converts. We planted the church almost two years ago and the Lord continues to bless it.

This Friday one of our members felt very uncomfortable about the man who had wandered in and sat next to her. Something in her spirit was troubled about him. A few minutes after the service started, his watch started beeping. The man stood up and slipped outside and our sister sleuth quietly followed him. Sister Sleuth was attired in full Sudanese regalia, and when she pulls her tobe (covering) around her face closely, it is difficult to catch a clear glimpse of her. As she hovered near the gentleman in question, a man sidled up to him and asked, "Have they arrived?" "Yes, they are here!" was the answer and then our informer slipped back into church.

The difficult thing about growing a congregation here in Sudan is the fact that we are never quite sure who the informers are. Whether beeping watches or betraying lips, the element of wonder is always with us.

Despite ongoing uncertainty, we are very excited about what God is doing through KCC. We ask that you pray with us that the Lord continues to have his way. It is our hope and prayer that God will use KCC in such a way that this city and nation will truly be both "shaken and stirred."

LAND OF WEEBLE WOBBLES

If my memory serves me correctly, the jingle for these formidable entertainers goes something like, "Weebles wobble but they don't fall down!"

I just returned from an excursion to the National Museum. A German educator and expert on northern Sudanese Ancient History gave a guided tour through the preserved frescoes, unearthed from their graves of sand. For about one thousand years, northern Sudan played host to a Christian people, and our sands now suffocate the ruins of hundreds of churches.

As we toured the museum, ooo-ing and ah-ing over all the frescoes of Christians, crosses, and Christ, a group of school children chattered in. They were all female, they all had the standard issue military fatigue uniform, and they all had a headscarf tightly bound under their chin. I watched in fascination as their teacher led them directly to the centerpiece of the exhibit: A large fresco accurately detailing the nativity of Christ and including northern Sudanese tribesmen as the shepherds that adored the God-child.

What irony! Dozens of Muslim children gazing at a testimony to the risen Lord. A testimony dug out from their very native soil. This desert land once housed a thriving Christian community. What did the Holy Spirit whisper while as yet moldable minds looked up at their ancestors worshiping Jesus?

Sudan has taken a knockout punch and has wobbled. We have been knocked down but not out. All around us we sense the momentum gathering for a rebound to Christ. This week a young Muslim woman bowed her knee before King Jesus. This month three Muslim men made the same confession of allegiance. What an excitement we feel in our hearts as we realize that Sudan will indeed rebound to her first love.

"Do not, I beseech you, be troubled about the increase of forces already in dissolution. You have mistaken the hour of night. It is already morning." – Mr. Belloc, as quoted in G. K. Chesterson's *Orthodoxy*.

LAND OF FLYING FISH

Many of you know that my parents were missionaries in Africa for over 25 years. One of the many advantages of being an MK is that you learn how to hustle the airport customs staff. My mother always packed a gimmick on top of the first trunk she opened and used it to amuse the customs officials. You know you have them if you can distract the grumpy Smurfs from searching to smiling.

When we returned to Sudan last year, my mother donated to our cause – the infamous singing fish Big Mouth Billy Bass. When we landed in Sudan with all our accessories, the first (and carefully marked) trunk I opened revealed bold Billy Bass "perched" proudly on top of all. We trotted him out and as soon as he wiggled and waggled for a startled audience, our safe and free passage through customs was assured.

Since then, Billy has occupied a place of honor on top of my office bookshelf. At least he did until the day before yesterday. Two days ago as I worked at my desk below 7-foot-high nosebleed seat Billy, he grew tired of sitting and inexplicably launched himself into space. I became aware of his odyssey when his travel arc collided with my head. Billy split my noggin open and he's now been grounded to a low-level file cabinet post.

Yesterday, a believer walked into my office and asked the reason for the welt on my head. I explained and she retorted, "God obviously wants to tell you something. Get out of your office and go catch fish. You are a fisherman. Go do it!"

"Ha, ha!" I said. "Ha, ha...he, he...hmm, hmm. Ouch!" I guess I had better go.

LAND OF JUST IS

Justice in Sudan is often reduced to something that "just is." There is a fatalistic resignation to the fact that life is not fair and there is no use crying about it. Two somber incidents reinforced this sadness to me last week.

Najwa is the widow of Muhammed Adam Ali Mohammed, who before his untimely death was my closest Muslim friend. The phone company that Mohammed worked for gave a generous gift to Najwa to the tune of $8,000, a fortune in this economic setting. A short-lived fortune it proved to be, as the family of the deceased swooped down and devoured the whole sum, leaving Najwa and her two fatherless infants with nothing. The family also took away her house and any other small resource she worked for. Last week Najwa sat on our couch with sad eyes and shrugged the injustice away.

The very same day revealed another tragic scenario south of us. A World Food Program (WFP) plane dropped food to starving Sudanese in the war zone. The very same airstrip that houses the relief effort airplanes is home to the military's high-altitude bombers and helicopter gun ships. All relief odysseys must register their flight plans with the government; therefore it is easy to pinpoint destinations and the inevitable gathering of the starving. Food was dropped and the innocent quickly gathered around it. Then out of the providential skies dropped a fully armed helicopter, hovering over the assembled throng, and rather than grain, it rained down death. Seventeen people were slaughtered and many others wounded. For years, this has been the way it "just is."

These two unconnected examples of injustice – one personal and one corporate – are merely a couple drawn from the millions that could be cited around the world at any given moment. Injustice is not restrained by immigration officials and it cannot be identified through security x-rays. Regardless of age, culture or socioeconomic status, injustice prowls around like a defiant and rabid lion.

What we cannot do is give in with Najwa to the paralyzing notion that wrong is the way things "just are." Let us not forget that we are representatives of King Jesus – the eternally just. May we never stop the fight, based on relationship with him, to stand for truth, honor, integrity, decency, compassion, equality and justice. May the battle be commenced in our own heart and carried to the school board, the town hall, the media, the printed page and the ballot box. Today, I pray that you have the courage to stand up for what is right and that you do so in a spirit that is representative of Jesus, Jesus the Just.

LAND OF AN EARFUL

Luke and Zack are quite the little scrappers. Luke will challenge, "Papa, let's wrestle!" As soon as he does, Zack assumes his "Hulk Hogan on the Beach" position, furrows his brow, flexes his muscles and growls. The throw-down begins and already I am getting the worst of it.

Recently, I was lying on my side, preoccupied with fending off the furious blows of Hurricane Luke, when suddenly I realized my ear was filling up with liquid. I turned violently only to have the power stream hit me in the face as Zack completed his Fido at the fire hydrant impersonation. There is more than one way to lose a wrestling match.

Our ears can be filled with all kinds of unwanted visitors: a badly warbled prayer call from the mosque, the news of a fallen comrade, gossip, criticism, self-pity, filthy humor and a litany of other less than wholesome voices which clamor for the opportunity of audio residence. We cannot control everything that is squirted into our ears, yet we can walk away, rather than stand there allowing the ideologies of a fallen world to rain down upon us.

As you wrestle your own adversaries, pint-size or Goliaths, may you have the grace to guard your ear gate and turn away from anything less than wholesome. Our ears and eyes are the gateways to our minds. They will either be channels of truth, honor, purity, loveliness and grace, or they will be the aqueducts through which the devil urinates into our brains.

The choice is up to us.

LAND OF THE DEAD

Not much that is communicated at three in the morning is of a jovial nature. Too early for our liking on this "Good" Friday morning, the jangling of the phone roused us from our slumber and gave us news of the death of a friend. I arrived at the hospital where the body was still warm. Sudanese hospitals are not much to visit – let alone die in.

Custom dictates an almost immediate burial, so the body was stuffed into the backseat of my double cab truck – head on the lap of the shocked mother, legs roughly spread over the lap of the solemn father and bare feet pressed up against the window pane, firmly enough to leave little grease marks.

The family lives on the outskirts of our sprawling city, but the police checkpoints presented no problem. They took one look at the dead feet pressing against the pane and waved us through. I asked the mother, a believer, if she would like a quiet ride or if she would prefer to listen to an Arabic cassette I had in the tape deck. She opted for company. I teared up as she tried to sing along with "And when I think, that God His son not sparing, sent Him to die, I scarce can take it in..."

As we sat in the moonlit courtyard, I thought about the deceased. She was 19 and she had just given birth to a baby daughter. For the first time in my life, I felt faith well up in me to pray for the dead. I walked over to her, laid my hands on her and asked Jesus to raise her from the dead. I saw her chest swell. My heart leaped as God answered my prayer.

He said, "No." Her chest swelled when one of the mourners shifted position on the bed of sisal rope. The body raised and then settled back into its rigid slumber. My heartbeat took a few minutes to regain original pace.

Death has been very real for us this Easter. It has birthed in us a longing for the Resurrection and a refreshed commitment to live out whatever days remain for us with passion and resolve. The death of a young friend has in a fresh way reminded us of incredible love – an eternal Father who sent a young Savior to die...for me, for you, for us. And one day we shall rise, dead feet and all. It is a day I increasingly long for.

LAND OF MEANING

The downside of being a visionary is that sometimes the dreaming and scheming can envelop your thoughts and schedule, and you find yourself always dwelling on the collective, never in personal witness. In the midst of ambitious plans, Jennifer and I have decided to focus our time and prayers this year on one family. We would like you to pray with us for them. They are our delightful Muslim neighbors, Mazhar and Intizaar, Ahmed, Ruya and Rana.

Three days ago my doorbell rang and I opened it to find Mazhar standing there with shining eyes. "I have got to tell you something. Something strange and wonderful has just happened!"

Mazhar went on to explain that 32 years ago when he was a teenager, he was swimming in the Nile. He felt something brush against his leg and it scared him. Reaching down into the water, he pulled up, to his astonishment, a wooden cross. "Thirty million people near this river and a cross finds its way to me?" He said that for two years this incident troubled him and he tried to think what God was telling him, but eventually he dismissed the incident from his mind.

That very day, he had been on his way home from work. "I felt Allah tell me to go home by a different way," he explained. And then with eyes glowing he said, "Look what I found!" He held up a wooden rosary, from which dangled a simple, elegant cross. "Here again in unusual circumstance God has brought a cross into my life. What in the world does that mean?"

It was obvious that God is answering our prayers for this family. I told Mazhar simply that I thought God wants him to follow the way of the cross and we have set another appointment to talk at length as to "what in the world" that means. At the end of our conversation, this tall, regal Arab clutched the cross tightly to him and said, "I am going to hurry home and tell my wife!"

Thank you for praying with us! The way of the cross surely does lead home.

LAND OF TOILETS

We have entered the season of electricity outages – never an eagerly anticipated time, especially when the temperature is consistently over 120 degrees. Last week the power went out in the evening and I went outside to start our generator. Looking over the cemetery, which slides up to our house, I could see one brightly lit building in the distance.

This building evidently had its own generator for it stood as a lighthouse in the communal dark. A toi-lighthouse, ironically enough. This five-story building is entirely devoted to the display of porcelain thrones. There are seats of marble with gold plated finishing, there are gaudy and extravagant stools of every color, and there are delicate and mysterious accessories of all natures and nationalities. Huge bay windows are built into the walls on all sides, so all who pass by can fill their vision with every form of toilet imaginable.

The whole building confuses me. Have these friends never heard of catalogues? Why not one display room with a few toilets (that could even double as benches and chairs, pots for plants, fountains, whatever) with a dozen catalogues? Why five floors of extravagant toilets when 95 percent of homes in the nation use the tried and true trusty hole in the ground? Why build a high-rise and furnish it, of all things, with Thomas Crapper's most infamous invention? Why waste so much money on a monument to non-essential extravagance? A city in darkness and the only light available illumines a potty.

This anomaly makes me question my own life. What five story idols have I erected in my own heart? What receptacle of waste have I exalted and lit for all to see? What non-essentials have I pampered, cultivated and dedicated time and money to? When I am proud of my limited natural abilities, when I invest in selfish ambition, when I blow my own trumpet and reverse up to people so they can pat me on the back – am I not in God's perspective building an altar of toilets? Do I not need my heart to be flushed? Do you?

LAND OF CHEWING

The Islamic month of Ramadan has chomped to a halt. The feast that celebrates the end of the fast has chewed itself still and life has returned to normal.

Most of you are aware that the Islamic style of fasting dictates a total abstinence from food, drink, cigarettes and sexual relations during the day – and the indulgent celebration of all the above by night. More food is consumed in Ramadan than in any other month. On a daily basis the fast is broken communally after the sunset prayer call – and I am always intrigued by the absolute silence of those first few minutes as juices are gulped down and delicious foods quickly ingested.

It has been a good Ramadan for our team here as we have participated in the fast as a means to witness. Here are some Ramadan news "bites":

- The team fasted with our Muslim contacts and broke the fast daily with them, sometimes in the street and sometimes in homes. We also hosted an evangelistic break-fast at sundown in which 15 seekers attended and the gospel was presented in a contextual manner.

- A Muslin man accepted the Lord during this time. He is growing in the Lord at an encouraging rate.
- One of our Muslim converts was asked by a group of Muslim colleagues to lead the prayers. He was able to use it as an opportunity to share about Christian faith and why we fast – drawing a positive comparison to the works-oriented fasting of Islam.
- Another Muslim convert has been sharing the gospel with the Imam of the local mosque. In one of the Friday sermons, this Imam preached to his mosque from the prophet Isaiah!
- Prayers are offered after every breaking of the fast. In order to communicate that followers of Jesus are also people of prayer, we would sit alongside our Muslim friends as they prayed. Facing a different direction, we would lift our hands and pray God's revelation upon them. Many significant and powerful gospel presentations were given.

Thank you for praying along with us continually for Sudan and her precious people. Ramadan reminds us again that the god of this world has deceived and bound them so tightly that unless the God of all worlds opens their eyes, there is no way for them to be saved. We ask that you continue to believe with us for a mass awakening and to look forward to the marriage break-fast of the Lamb.

LAND OF APPOINTMENTS

Tomorrow morning I am supposed to meet with the Minister of the Interior. We have been without a visa now for almost two months and this man has the authority to end the impasse. Thank you for your ongoing prayers.

As important as that appointment is, it pales when compared

to others. Our neighbor and friend suffered a massive heart attack, and at four o'clock this morning passed on to meet his Maker. The last few hours have been spent grieving with his family, carrying the shroud-wrapped body on our shoulders to the cemetery, offering tearful prayers with the men of the community, and resting the corpse on his right side, facing east.

As we stood around the grave, I looked down at the sand where my distinct sandal print mingled with that of friends and neighbors. It reminded me of the awesome privilege I and my family have to live, laugh, mourn and die among our Sudanese friends. More so, to remind them that "it is appointed unto men once to die, and then the judgment."

Though I do not know the deceased's final choice, I know he did not lack opportunity. Two weeks ago we invited him to a breaking of the Ramadan fast in which we clearly presented the gospel.

We do not need to be ashamed when Muslims choose not to respond to the gospel message. Once a Muslim has heard and understood, he is accountable for his own choice. Let us be ashamed if we have not declared the message. Let us be ashamed if we are not integrated into the community. Let us be ashamed if we have not learned Arabic well. Let us be ashamed if we are not knowledgeable about culture. Let us be ashamed if we garble the message. Let us be ashamed if we have not developed calluses on our collective knees. We have been appointed to proclaim. May we simply do our duty.

Five minutes ago a Muslim convert walked into my office beaming. In the meeting on Friday, he was astonished to see his cousin sitting two rows in front of him. From the same family, two men, without knowing of the other, have made the choice to follow Jesus. What joy these two new disciples shared together – appointed together to life eternal!

LAND OF IMMUNITY

I walked in the house the other day to see my son Zack sitting in the corner and waving something in the face of his friend. They sat there giggling while Zack pressed this thing to his own mouth and then to the mouth of his compadre. On closer inspection the object proved to be a large, plump and very dead mouse. Earlier in the week, Jennifer walked in on Zack as he merrily sat watching TV while licking the toilet brush. We are fairly confident that he is building up his immunities and will be a supremely healthy adult!

You have been praying with us about our visa. We were relying on two men of influence to help us meet the authorities that could override our expulsion. One, our neighbor and an ambassador, suffered the shock of his beloved brother dying from a massive heart attack. We set up an appointment with the other and on the way to the appointment he had an accident and his Mercedes was smashed. We re-scheduled the appointment only to have that date missed as he was called urgently out of town on unexpected business. It became increasingly evident that "someone" does not want us here.

Christmas Eve found me sitting in the State Minister for Foreign Affairs office. He listened to our problem, kindly offered to help, and summoned an aid to write us a letter granting us a one-year visa and multiple exit/reentry! Praise the Lord! The visa is not yet in the passport, but the edict has been made. Junior officers are dragging their feet, but it is only a question of when, not if. Thank you for your prayers. What a timely Christmas present! When we are in the will of the Lord and under his protection, we are immune from all the fiery darts slung against us.

When Jesus came to this earth in lowly form, he guaranteed our immunity. Free from the curse of sin, free from the fear of death, free to live eternally. We are free to love, free to serve, free to forgive. Our junior enemies may grumble and drag their feet, but the edict has been made and the end sure, "You shall call his name Jesus, for he shall save his people from their sins!"

LAND OF LITTLE

It is simply fantastic to breathe the dust-filled air of Sudan again. (If you are a nose picker, then Sudan is your paradise!) We arrived back after three whirlwind weeks in the U.S.

While driving through Ohio two weeks ago, Jennifer and I were bemused to see a huge billboard stretching across a rolling hill just outside Cincinnati. The loud yellow letters proclaimed, "CHARLIE'S TATTOO PARLOR – DONE WHILE YOU WAIT." I can imagine Charlie saying, "All right, Nellie, that will be $27.50. If you'll leave your right arm here and come back in half an hour, your purple dragon will be ready!"

We are not very good at waiting – tattoos, guidance, deliverance and even delays on little answers – all stretch our patience. We want BIG and we want NOW. This morning I read two verses from Deuteronomy 4 that seem appropriate for Sudan: "The Lord your God will drive out those nations before you little by little. You will be unable to destroy them at once.... But the Lord your God will inflict defeat upon them until they are destroyed"(verses 22 and 23, emphasis added).

Islam is a gangrene giant. It is doomed, but it will not fall like Goliath; it will slowly rot away. Thank you for your patience. Thank you for little prayers, little offerings, little encouragements and little faiths. Thank you for believing and waiting with us.

Some "little" testimonies:

* Our first house church is flapping like mad and about ready for lift off.
* A seeker from western Sudan is almost found.
* Today we closed the contract for the ladies teahouse (outreach center). We will remodel and equip this month to hopefully open by April 1.

LAND OF (HELL'S) BELLS

John Donne warned us not to ask "for whom the bell tolls," as we might not like the answer. There have been bells tolling this past week and I have not enjoyed their thunder. The most harmless was my 33rd birthday bell (I am now into bonus time), but the others were not so pleasant.

Priscilla is a Kenyan who has been working as a teacher here in Sudan. Sometime ago, she married a Sudanese who had converted to Christianity. Then several months ago, her husband was arrested by security and repeated efforts could not locate him. Her house was ransacked and looted, and Priscilla moved twice, seeking safety. Now several weeks ago, Priscilla also disappeared.

The telephone (bell) rang at the school where Priscilla was employed, and an informant asked the headmaster to come to the hospital to retrieve her battered body. The official line is that she was killed in a car accident; the reality is much sinister. Her husband has not yet been found.

Another bell wailed for a 48-year-old neighbor of ours who passed away suddenly, leaving young children behind. She was a Muslim and now lies in storage, waiting for both temporal and eternal worms.

My neighbor Mahmoud is 85 and failing. I spent time with him and his wife again yesterday, and after I had shared Jesus, he said in a voice that I could hardly understand for its weakness, "I just cannot accept that Jesus is the only Savior." The bell signaling the end of his bout is just about to clang.

I have mentioned it before, so please forgive the repetition. My favorite Christmas hymn is "Joy to the World." Allow me to misquote a longed-for line, "He comes to make his (bell)essings known... far as the curse is found." As far, as wide, as long as the cursed bell of human mortality and tragedy tolls – to that extent and beyond – Jesus has come to make his salvation known. So in the words of another Christmas carol, "Come on ring those bells! Everybody sing, 'Jesus is the King, born for you and me.....'"

Thank you for praying for us, that we would out-ring even the best Salvation Army Santa. May you likewise neither falter nor fail. When our bell tolls for our time is "donne," may our arms be withered and broken from constant ringing.

LAND OF MISSILES

For all of us, these are interesting days, not knowing what will fall out of the sky on our heads. The demonstrations here in Sudan have heated up over the last few days with angry crowds rain-ing bricks and stones down on both police and expatriates. One English friend had her car smashed by an angry mob. A Dutch friend had petrol poured on his car and was only just able to drive away before the fuel was ignited. Black clouds of smoke have billowed over the city for the last two days.

Jennifer had to dodge her own lethal projectile this week. She walked into one of the local grocery stores to find two men trying to kill a large rat that had crawled up out of the sewer. Their method of "shock and awe" was to drop kick the rat to its eternity. As an innocent civilian, Jennifer tried to peacefully exist in the strife of that battle zone, but the rat was booted airborne directly at her. It flew at her face but sped by, teeth shining, centimeters from her nose.

All sorts of nasty things have been hurled at us recently. To be American (let alone, missionary) is to currently bear the wrath of many nations – European and Arab. The Iraqi war has consumed our attention, but it will eventually fly past us with teeth exposed. The war for men's souls will go on. As the devil continues to fling his da(rats) at us here in Sudan, we continue to covet your prayers. We want to stand firm and kind in the face of all projectiles – earthly and demonic – for the sake of these lost sheep Jesus loves so intensely.

LAND OF SELFISH GIVERS

Last week we visited an Arab friend who just returned from three years in Egypt. As is common these days, the conversation turned to Iraq and America's foreign policy. I have become somewhat weary of these conversations of late, since most of them are very emotive and angry. This conversation was different. The whole family really was struggling through their pain to understand.

Saadiq said, "America is like a friend who comes to your house and showers you with gifts and then comes back two weeks later and tells you how to raise your children and treat your wife. We are thankful for the many good things from America, but their intrusive arrogance is very difficult for us to accept."

His perceptive comment made me think of my own philosophy of giving and that of my nation. I love to give when I love to give. At other times I make Scrooge look beneficent. America too can be incredibly generous – but on her own terms and often with strings attached.

Have you ever noticed that some of the most selfish people are great givers? When a cause aligns with their agenda, they can pour out their time, resources and energy. I am a selfish giver, generously biased, for when I am approached with a need outside of my radar, I am calloused and unresponsive. In my own context, some of the most emotionally and spiritually needy are the very ones that rub me the wrong way.

Perhaps you would feel free enough to join me in a prayer:

> Lord, I love to give when I love to give
> But when unmoved
> I am hard.
> Please help me to give to those that try me, annoy me and displease me.
> Please free me from the shackles of selfish generosity.

LAND OF ANTI

It seems to me that to be anti-war is oxymoronic. War involves forces at opposition and the collision of opinions and agendas. War is the state of being anti. Therefore, to protest war is basically to say, "I am anti being anti!" Not a very tenable position. Violence is the fruit, apposition the root.

There is no doubt that here in Sudan we are at war. It is a war we eagerly participate in, for we are striving with God for the souls of Muslim men and women. Our first house church of Muslim background believers is gelling nicely. It is so encouraging to see the continual process of maturation right before our eyes. We are winning the battle for these souls (another this last week accepted the lordship of King Jesus), but not without resistance.

One friend (let us call him Matthew) has been in a firefight. Security has been following him recently and last week confronted his family. They told his Muslim parents that Matthew had become a follower of Jesus. Matthew's father, a determined

Sufi mystic, said, "If this is true, I will kill him myself!" The other relatives accosted Matthew, slapped him around, abused him verbally and gave him two days to recant. Matthew is standing firm, anticipating testifying of his Lord through baptism and even telling others about the Way, the Truth and the Life.

The other church members are also embracing this gently serious war. It thrills us to see them reaching out to their families and friends with the gospel. It has been seven long years here, but we are beginning to see the ripple effect.

Would you pray with us, that the Holy Spirit would continue to empower us to be anti-death, anti-deception, anti-selfish and anti-lazy, and pro-Jesus, pro-eternal life, pro-truth and pro-proclamation?

LAND OF PASTOR IMAM

Last week in our house church gathering, we each took turns talking about a Muslim that we would love to see God reel in. After each person was described, we prayed as a group that he would be fished. One of our members named Maajid asked that we pray for the leader of an Islamic group that a year ago had invited him to come and speak to them.

This group seemed to be unusual in the fact that their questions were not framed to disprove Christianity but rather to discover truth. They soaked up the answers and eagerly accepted the literature and Scriptures that were offered. Then they disappeared off the radar.

Until we prayed.

Two days later on a "chance" encounter (i.e. divine appointment), Maajid bumped into this Islamic leader in a bookstore. "I have been looking for you all over!" he said. "All of my people are fascinated with Jesus and are asking me all kinds of questions that I do not know how to answer. I have become their Jesus-Imam. Can you get me the Jesus film so that I have a resource to answer all of their questions?" Of course, with delight, Maajid provided the requested film.

Thank you for your prayers for Muslims and their extended

communities. We are moving ever closer to bursting nets and see over-laden boats. Please continue to pray for this group; they are definitely in process. Pray that the Seeker of their souls would help them navigate all the hidden reefs and pounding surf to the haven of eternal rest.

LAND OF LACK
About two years ago, we noticed the lack of focus we had as a Sudanese team on children. As a result two ministries have been launched. One is a school and the other an English club. The focus of both is to minister to Muslim children and their parents.

A few weeks ago, a little Muslim girl went home singing what she learned that day in class: "God our Father, God our Father, we thank you, we thank you, for our many blessings...." That evening her mother, a devout Muslim, called up our administrator and said, "Please do not teach our daughter to sing that terrible song... Nowhere in the Qur'an is God described as 'Father.'" Technically she is right. There is a total lack of the concept of the Father heart of God in Islamic theology. It is Jesus who makes the Fatherhood of God a reality. Our team was able to visit this family and explain.

A week ago in one of the English clubs, the Muslim children were asked to imagine what the world would look like in 30 years. One six-year-old piped up, "I hope that in 30 years all the Christians are killed and Islam rules the world." This otherwise delightful young man lacks a little bit of perspective.

The longer we live among Muslims, the more we love these wonderful people and grieve over their essential lack: Jesus. Missing Jesus, they miss everything. First John 5:12, "He who has [Jesus] has life; he who does not have [Jesus] does not."

Please pray with us. Pray that those so ignorant of their primary lack would find him and, finding him, be embraced by the Father.

LAND OF COVER
"Harry" is a fourth-year law student at the main university in town. I was introduced to him through one of our Muslim background

believers. Harry was struggling with fear and lack of certainty that Islam can guarantee heaven. We began studying the Bible together and Harry was ravenous. One day I dropped in unexpectedly at the university to visit him. I was encouraged to see that he was covertly carrying around his Bible; it was covered by a colorful poster given out by a local pharmacy. I was embarrassed to note that the poster in bold letters was advertising a cream for the treatment of "Vaginitis." Sometimes ignorance is bliss!

Sometimes it is not. Not when life and death are on the line. This Monday, I am happy to tell you – and I would crow it from the rooftop if I could – Harry crossed from ignorance into assurance. In the candlelight of our 120-degree living room, Harry took one last glance at the heat of hell and stepped out of doubt into the covering shade of Jesus.

The Saturday prior, another Muslim also stepped into the shadow of the Savior. This man had a succession of dreams. First he dreamt he met Mohammed in the desert. As he approached him, Mohammed vaporized, as if to denote he had nothing to offer. Next he dreamt about the Pharaohs, who in all their splendor could not cover him. In his final dream, a shining cross was placed around his neck.

For days this man could not sleep and finally approached his father. "I am going crazy. Please can I approach some Christians and ask them what this means?" His father said, "Well, it seems that it is better that you go to them than for you to die." This man approached one of our team and, after much earnest conversation, stepped from the sun to the Son. His sins are covered. He and Harry are home free!

Over the last six months, we have seen six Muslim men accept the covering of Jesus. What wonder! What joy! What promise! Some day soon these holes in the dyke are going to merge and we will see living water flow, covering all this thirsty land.

LAND OF BOTTOM
It is a joy to watch my family grow. The prayers of the boys are a particular delight, even if they sometimes leave me a little red-

faced. In the presence of company last week, little Luke fervently pleaded:

> Dear God,
> Thank you for making the trees and the flowers and the ocean.
> Please help Papa not to be naughty…and not to touch Mamma's bottom.
> Amen!

Another memorable encounter of last week concerned a fellow missionary at the bottom of the pay scale. This young single missionary woman mentioned in passing that because of the Iraqi conflict, there had been an adjustment in the support she receives monthly. She is merrily continuing her ministry: working with imprisoned children, teaching at a rural Bible School, ministering in a local church all to the tune of $197 per month… total. She could not be happier and is not seeking additional support.

These diverse encounters prompt two thoughts:

1) The view from the bottom is not as bad as it's cracked up to be.
2) May we all be grateful for the generous way that God takes care of us.

We are grateful to you for the part you play in our financial and prayer support. We are well provided for and thank you… from the bottom of our hearts!

LAND OF IMMANENCE

"Jesus is coming soon!" boomed the preacher to a sea of nodding heads. "We must be ready to stand before him on judgment day" to a few muted "Amens." "No one knows when Jesus will return; thus we must live a life worthy of him" to somber silence.

It is not often that you watch a sermon on the second return of Christ broadcast on Sudanese national TV. It is even less often that the sermon saunters forth from the mouth of an Imam who presides over the pulpit of one of the most fundamentalist of mosques.

Though correct on a portion of his theology, this Imam is still off center. He went on to preach that Jesus will come to implement the sharia (law) of Mohammed. As I drove by his mosque this week with a Muslim background believer (MBB), the believer said to me, "Do you see that tall minaret there? It reminds me of Islam: straight on the outside but inside crooked and curled."

The warning of this Imam seemed prophetic this morning as a Sudanese Airways airplane crashed killing all on board (116), save one two-year-old boy.

All of us better be ready to meet Jesus. Whether it be a confused Imam, an airline tragedy or the sad face of a neighbor dragging himself off to work that reminds us, may we all be reminded that Jesus is coming soon. Some of us will meet him sooner – and in the meantime the nations perish all around us.

LAND OF ROADBLOCKS

As in many countries in this part of the world, police roadblocks are set up after midnight on all the primary intersections. Drivers are flagged down and examined, usually by sleepy-eyed officers. Other roadblocks are not so passive.

A Christian returned in despair from his interview. Across his application a red ink rejection had been scrawled, "There is no job for you because you are a Christian."

An outreach team some time ago broke down in the desert of western Sudan. Afraid for their lives, because of their proximity to bandits, they began to pray, bind the evil spirits and rebuke the devil for allowing them to break down. Two other cars passed within hailing distance but refused to stop and help despite the pleas of the stranded. The fearful group went to bed that night discouraged and upset.

Oddly enough in the morning, they were able to start the car immediately. They proceeded down the road to find the two cars that had abandoned them destroyed and the drivers killed. To quote a team member, "We had been binding the will of God. We thought it was the enemy that made us breakdown when actually it was God's protection. Our breakdown was God's roadblock."

There is another inscription written in red across the cross-roads of time. It is the ink of Calvary blood – and it both protects and enables. I am thankful for the blood of Jesus, which affirms our eternal application that we are accepted into the King's family.

May we also be discerning enough to accept God's road-blocks in our lives and not waste our energies "binding" what he has lovingly ordained.

LAND OF SPIT

It would be a stretch to say that my boys Luke and Zack are a spitting image of me, but we could settle for images with spit.

Sudanese, especially women, love to squeeze the cheeks of children they think are cute. My midget men, being 113 percent male, hate to have their cheeks squeezed by women who are cooing "sweetie." Last week Zack struck a blow back for the little guys. We were at the airport together and he had just taken a large swig of water. Rather than immediately swallowing, he kept the water in billowed-out cheeks. A passing lady could not resist his cute little face and bent down to his level to give him the big squeeze. As thanks for her labors, she received a face full.

Luke had his own spit experience this week but on the receiving end. Luke is very athletic and already aware of the food that is good for him – like carrots for the eyes – while Zack makes the cookie monster look refined. This week some rascally street kids were passing by our house and spit into the eyes of Luke. He was remarkably unperturbed merely saying to Jennifer, "Mom, some street kids just spit in my eyes. Please bring me some carrots."

The reality of life as a disciple of Jesus includes getting squeezed and spit on. In this age our eyes are especially assaulted. There is so much filth in the public forum that we are continually bombarded with messages less than healthy for us. We would all do well – when squeezed and spit upon – not to howl and scratch another mark on the barrel of our victim hood, but to softly turn to Jesus and ask for a carrot – the carrot of his word, the carrot of his face, the carrot of what is pure, true, noble and wholesome. Above all, let us not stand in line unblinking before the broadcast filth of the world waiting for spit in our eyes, but let us "fix our eyes on Jesus, the author and perfector of our faith." And being half-Greek I stand with my kin and say, "Sir, we would see Jesus."

LAND OF PRESENCE

We have been encouraged in recent months at the spiritual growth we see in the house church. The numbers are down a little bit (three of our members fled the country – two to Egypt and one to Dubai), but thanks be to God for he never flees.

Last Saturday we met in one of the member's homes. We meet every Saturday but always in a different home to avoid security being able to identify a pattern. The format of a usual meeting includes a time of fellowship and eating, prayer and praise, and then Bible teaching. This meeting followed the pattern with one exception. At the end of the teaching time, the presence of God was incredibly tangible. For a half hour no one moved, flinched or blinked. We sat soaking in Jesus.

Two days later, I bumped into one of the members in the street. He was still glowing. "I love Jesus and His message so much," he said. "He is in my blood!"

The pace of our lives and ministries does not often lend itself to extended soaking. The format of our worship services tends to lean towards activity and commotion. Often this activity is productive, but let us also look forward to – and enjoy – times of great stillness in the presence of Jesus. Let us allow him to permeate into our blood.

LAND OF DREAMS

Hassan is a dear friend and believer in Jesus. Two weeks ago his wife Suad (who is still a Muslim) approached him and asked him to listen to her dream. Hassan gave a Bertie Wooster laugh (firing on only one tonsil) and brushed her off. He felt that often her dreams were frivolous and uninspiring. This time she persisted, and eventually he broke down and agreed to listen.

I am glad he did because the dream was full of powerful Biblical imagery. In her dream the family (Hassan, Suad and their two young boys Sammy and Salim) was driving the car and being chased by sinister men in a black car. No matter which way they turned the car followed them. As they tried in vain to escape they found themselves trapped between the dark car and a looming, unending, impassible wall. Suad became frantic for the only passage through the wall was a very narrow door. There was no way their car could fit through it in the natural – but somehow they did and escaped the black car.

On the other side of the wall, they encountered a desert landscape of valleys, canyons, boulders, again impossible for the car to pass. But again somehow they began to make their way though the obstacles. As they passed a huge tree with spreading branches, one of the branches grabbed Suad by the hair while Hassan and the boys drove on. She struggled and eventually freed herself, following on foot. She eventually entered a land full of milk and honey and found Hassan and the boys reclining in peace and comfort. Suad looked around at the tranquil scene and then woke up.

Hassan was so excited when he told me of the dream, and he asked me what it meant. Even though I have no colored coat and have never been closeted up with lions, the meaning seemed pretty evident: The unrelenting pursuit of sin and the huge wall of separation between sin and safety only being passed through the narrow door Jesus. The reality of deliverance from sin is the beginning not the culmination, as after we are saved we still live and move in a world of challenge and obstacle. The sobering fact that no spouse can ride his/her partner's convertible to glory and that faith presides over family.

Suad's dream ended on a note of promise. Hassan is confident that Suad will find her way (as we all must do), and that as a family they will enjoy Jesus and heaven forever. We believe with him. Would you believe with us?

Many Muslims are drawn to Jesus through dreams and visions. Please continue to pray with us that dreams will lead to searching, and searching to finding.

LAND OF LIPS

One of the pleasures of serving in Sudan is the spirit of unity and cooperation between missions groups. Last week I was invited to speak at the annual conference of the Leprosy Mission. These dear saints work in some of the most remote regions of Sudan among society's outcasts. I spoke on what it meant to really be a disciple of Jesus, not just a follower rendering lip service.

One of the Sudanese ladies responded with this story:

"One day God called a lion to the throne room and pointed out a certain village. ' Do you see that village?' God asked the Lion, 'Those are my people. I forbid you to eat any of them.' The lion agreed and went his sauntering way. Some time later the Lion entered the village and ate every resident. God again called the Lion saying, 'I thought that I told you not to eat any of the residents of that village. They all were my people!' The Lion responded, 'Oh, I am so sorry. I started to eat them at their feet, and I did not get any whiff of you until I reached their lips.'"

May we be disciples down to our toes. May our feet, hands and extremities honor Jesus. May our feet be going feet, our hands giving hands and may our very being be the aroma of Jesus. It is interesting to note that one of the first parts of the body affected by leprosy is the lips. God is not very interested in beautiful lips – unless they move in harmony with an obedient life.

LAND OF TESTIMONY

We are now well into the month of Ramadan and the city has taken on a lazy/sleepy feel. While many aspects of Ramadan are oppressive, others are opportune. There are wonderful opportunities to share the breaking of the fast daily with friends and neighbors, and we always have a window to present Jesus in these times. Yesterday I was in a desert town four hours north of the capital. After breaking the fast we reclined on the mats in the dusty streets and sipped on the obligatory mint tea. In the cozy warmth of the post sunset, we were able to clearly testify of

"Christ crucified" to our listening hosts.

Islam is the only major religion that denies this central fact of our faith. I find it more and more urgent to testify to these truths. In this age when clever lips would distort and meld all faiths into one ineffectual fog, how desperately needed is the voice which calls out with Paul, "We testify that Christ died for our sins according to the Scriptures, that he was buried, that he rose on the third day according to the scriptures, and that he was seen by [many witnesses]!"

This week, I also received a moving testimony from a Muslim background believer. This dear brother has fled Sudan to Egypt, but this is what he writes: "I want to come back to Sudan to preach Jesus... I have a good job here in Egypt, but I realize that I do not need money. I need Jesus, the Lord of Heaven. I love Jesus so much."

Testifying of Jesus will not always make us popular, but it is our duty and our honor to lift Jesus up daily – so that those who will may be drawn to him.

LAND OF THANKSGIVING

Tomorrow is the last day of Ramadan and since it is culturally acceptable to be thankful this week... I am duly so. Ramadan has its positive moments: the communal aspect of breaking the fast in the street, the extended visitation, the holiday feast, and the collective sigh of relief when it's all over.

But it is also a month in which we invariably sleep fitfully and argue incessantly. Though the Islamic tradition states that in Ramadan all the demons of hell are bound and the angels of heaven released, we have found it to be experientially the opposite.

Ramadan makes me thankful that I belong to Jesus.

Immediately after breaking the fast, my Muslim friends will rearrange the reed mats and perform the sunset prayers. We usually sit or kneel behind them, lift our hands and intercede for them. Last week, Zack climbed on my lap and began a loud play-by-play of the prostrations:

"Look, Papa, at all the Muslims praying...."
"Papa, do you see all these Muslims?"
"They are all going to hell."
"Papa, hell is hot."
"We need to tell all these Muslims about Jesus."

Since some of my Muslim friends understand English, I wondered what they were thinking as they listened to Zack's factual commentary and tried to concentrate on their prayers. I did not stop him. In fact, it is one of the few times I wished he had a volume button that I could have turned UP!

We wish you a blessed Thanksgiving. We will miss sharing the turkey with you but are eternally glad that we can partake together of Jesus. There are so many others who do not even know what they are missing.

LAND OF SLEEP TALKERS

Some dear friends recently lost a baby to miscarriage. Because they could not afford a private hospital for the necessary operation, they found themselves in a ward with seven Muslim women. As our friend started to slowly awake from the anesthesia, she began to pray in a loud voice, not yet conscious of what she was saying nor her surroundings, "Jesus, save the Muslim people! Jesus reveal yourself as the only way, the only truth, the only life!"

Her husband smiled to himself and was proud of his semi-conscious intercessor – until she cranked the volume up and started to blast, "And show them that Mohammed is a liar and a fraud. Let them realize he is like the antichrist...."

And thus her husband was cast into a dilemma. It is not really kosher to muzzle a spouse emerging into consciousness, yet he did not want to be stoned to death by the lumpy pillows of seven bed-ridden Muslim women either.

Dudley Woodberry mentioned in a lecture that the Islamic crescent moon symbol is quite apropos: The crescent moon is not a source of light. It is only a reflection of the sun source. Further, it is dark in the core.

I often feel that Muslim people are sleepwalking through life. They have a measure of reflected truth, but it frames a dark vacuum. Would you pray with us for our Sudanese Muslim friends and for Muslims around this orb? Pray that they would awake from their slumber and find their reality in Jesus.

LAND OF SHUT UP

Recently my father was driving down the road in Jerusalem with a missionary from Papua New Guinea. Her name is Heidi and she is quite the peppy prayer warrior. As they drove, the nearby minaret launched its audio assault: "Alllllllllahu Akbar..." Heidi abruptly responded, "SHUT UP IN THE NAME OF JESUS!" and immediately the prayer call ceased. My dad checked that he was not speeding, had his seat belt on, and had no current sin in his life... you never can be too careful with one of those prophet types as a passenger!

This week in our ladies community center, a Muslim woman came in. She was distraught over a relationship gone wrong and had visited a local sheikh for a cure. Many of these sheikhs delve into the demonic. This lady collapsed on the ground, writhing and screaming in torment. Our staff gathered around her and rebuked the demons in the name of Jesus. They were able to minister to this tormented soul.

In this our 10th year of working among Muslims, we are convinced more than ever of the impotence of human wisdom and technique against the bondages of Islam. We now understand culture, speak Arabic and have constant opportunities to witness to our Muslim friends, and yet the answer is not culture or language or friendship as much as these things help. Jesus is the answer. Unless he breaks the bondage around Muslim souls and minds, they remain bound. We look forward with you to more anointed "Shut ups!" Increasingly Jesus penetrates through the darkness of Islam and the result is a liberating release.

This seems to be a common hope in our home these days. Little Zack (age 4) was sitting in front of the TV/Video this morning and Jennifer heard him address it, "Shut up in the name of

Jesus!" And to that we all say a hearty "Amen!"

LAND OF WOMEN

I have always wondered what it would be like to be a fundamentalist Muslim woman. A few months ago a temptation a(veiled) itself that I found impossible to flee. Jennifer and I were invited to a farewell party for a lady leaving Sudan and we were instructed to come in costume. Borrowing Jennifer's hijaab (long black robe), I added black socks, shoes and complete veil and sauntered into the party as an imposing 6'3" blackened maiden. I walked around the room and pinched the rears of all my male friends taking great delight in their startled reactions. It was a challenge to eat however, and I left that party thankful to be a man and relieved I had not been booted out of the country for cross dressing (it probably would not have gone over well with you, our sending constituency).

One of our colleagues received a telephone call this week from a Muslim woman who wanted desperately to meet in person. At the hour of the appointment, horrific back pain struck our colleague and she almost postponed the appointment. She decided to grit through and was ecstatic at the result. As these two women sat studying the Scripture, tears began to poor from the Muslim woman's eyes as she confessed, "I have been so hungry." Right there she accepted Jesus as Lord!

Another woman (a secret believer) was exposed in her Islamic University when she defended the authenticity of the Bible with a little too much veracity. The administration of the school told her she must give a lecture (scripted for her), which basically denied the Bible, the Cross and the Christ. After prayer she gave the lecture but spurned the script. To the shock of her hearers, she spoke boldly of her love for Jesus and her trust in his word. Being a little spunky she is applying to be reinstated to the University.

Though I am glad to be a man, I thank God for women. Not only are they turning to Jesus and standing up for him, there are more female missionaries in Sudan then men. This is both a credit to them and a shame to my (usual) gender. Long live women!

LAND OF PASSION

I am not quite sure what happened to Mel Gibson 12 years ago, but I love the fruit. We hear so many encouraging testimonies from the States regarding The Passion of the Christ. Allow me to share some from this neck of the desert.

In Jordan the film is selling to packed houses: you have to purchase tickets days in advance and the usual response is a standing ovation. In Cairo, Dubai and Doha, Muslims are flooding to the theaters. In Iran, the leading cleric is calling for the film to be allowed publicly. In Kuwait, there is a movement to allow the film to be shown to general audiences.

Last night we invited 30 friends to join us for a viewing and discussion. A Malaysian Muslim ironically supplied us with a DVD version of the film. (When it comes to movies whose legality is of suspect nature, we are Clintonites: "Don't ask. Don't tell.") We met at the home of one of the richest Sudanese businessmen.

The evening was full of irony. I sat watching Jesus suffer between two of my friends – both named Mohammed. I had a secret stash of Bibles in the car in case the discussion went well. Mohammed to my right had a stash of alcohol in case the evening went "wrong." The owner of the house was also named Mohammed. Mohammed to my left became increasingly convicted as the passion unfolded. He began to groan and moan and cover his face. His body rocked and twitched. I was not sure he was going to make it.

After the compelling resurrection scene, we began to discuss the film. Some of the Muslims were visibly moved. Some argued that Jesus really did not die, believing rather that God switched bodies placing a look-alike on the cross. No one wanted to leave and as the discussion progressed we were able to share a very clear gospel message. The Mohammed to my left gripped my hand as he departed and said, "I have GOT to talk to you!"

What a wonderful tool this film has become. What delicious irony that the film no major studio wanted to market is being gobbled up around the world. How wonderful that Muslims are standing in line to see it. Whatever their initial reaction, the fact is that now a crucified Christ and the gospel core have been imprinted on their brains and hearts. What fodder for the Holy Spirit to refer to in dreams, dialogue and future decisions.

Gracias, Gibson. Glory to God!

LAND OF OBSERVERS

This part of the world is no stranger to observers. Periodically we invite them or endure them as they observe elections, genocides and the occasional half-clothed civilian who returns their curious stare.

James is a friend of mine, a pastor from southern Sudan, who this week had his fill of observers. He was invited to pray for a lady who had been paralyzed for three years. He entered the room and began to pray for her, when he heard the shuffling of feet and the muttering of voices. He looked up to see a gaggle of observing young evangelists waiting to see what would happen. Their observation sans participation angered him and so he threw them all out. One old woman poked her head in the door and said, "Pastor, I have the faith to pray with you!" Together they laid hands on the cripple and after 10 minutes of prayer, she leaped to her feet and went dancing down the dusty street.

Sudan is on the threshold of change. Peace documents are about to be smudged, while in the West lives continue to be snuffed out. Many are watching, observing.

If I may challenge you on the outside looking in...we need you now. Your kindly glances are encouraging, but not enough. We need your active presence. Pastors have a difficult time in Sudan. They are used to public preaching – which is not on the "Top Ten Things the Sudanese Government Endorses" list. We need lay people. If you are an educator – Nile Valley Academy is in constant need of teachers. If you can string to sentences of English together – we could use you in our Adult Education Center as an English Conversation partner or teacher. Come for two months, a year, two years, or a life.

You will not regret it.

LAND OF ANSWERS

This weekend a peace agreement was signed for Sudan. There has been great celebration here as many feel this is an answer to prayer. God is so amazing in his stewardship of nations and nobodies. He answers them all. These last two weeks we have had the privilege of hosting a team of students from Valley Forge Christian College. The team was amazing and God both blessed them and through them.

On one of the days the team was ministering at a center for street children. The center is run by wonderful Sudanese Christians and it caters to young boys in hopeless situations. After a long day, the center offered to share a meal with the team. Little did we know the center was out of food and that we consumed the children's last meal. We drove off unwittingly happy and the directors of the center gathered for prayer. Francis, the administrator, prayed out in faith, "Lord, you see we have no food for the children. I pray that you send some right now." As he finished praying, a truck rumbled into the "Boys Hope Center" laden with more than enough food to go around.

We are thankful that God is answering prayers for Sudan. Thank you for the prayers you have hurled toward heaven on our behalf. Rejoice with us that the Lord has answered and is answering.

Speaking of answers, I have two questions for you:

1) Sudan has evolved to a place that we are now able to receive certain types of teams. If your church is interested in sending a team, would you please consider contacting me? Groups should be college-age and above.

2) The work here has grown to the place that we really need a business manager. If you are a married man in your 30s or 40s and have skills in business plus a heart for Muslim people, would you please pray about coming as a missionary to Sudan? We desperately need you to manage our ever-expanding platform (five different platforms currently and eight by the end of the year). I am a vision-

ary, not a detail person. We need someone to take us to the next level, someone who can improve our efficiency in business operation, so that our credibility remains high in the community. It is from these platforms that we proclaim Jesus.

LAND OF SPIT FORGIVEN

In Sudan, as in many Middle Eastern countries of late, there are banners hanging in the street that Betsy Ross would not approve of. In the capital this week, prominently displayed on a major road, was a banner that read in English: AMERICAN KILLERS GO HOME. WE CAN SOLVE OUR OWN PROBLEMS. The sign referred to the Darfur province of Western Sudan and the recent visit of U.S. Secretary of State Colin Powell.

This summer we have enjoyed several outstanding interns and short-term workers from various churches. One of them, Robert, is, as you will see, the spitting image of his Father. The time had come for Robert to take leave of the Muslim students he had been teaching in our English center. One man he had grown close to walked him to the bus station and there they embraced in farewell. A militant Muslim observed the affection between American Christian and Sudanese Muslim and, enraged, spit on them. The Sudanese friend was incensed, but immediately Robert grabbed his hands, looked directly into his eyes and said, "Forgive him."

The Sudanese went home that night and tossed and turned on his bed, unable to sleep. "How can this American Christian have the gut reflex of forgiveness? He did not have time to think. He just responded. It was in his character to forgive. How can that be?"

This same Sudanese watched The Passion of the Christ film in our house this week and was moved to tears at Jesus forgiving the ones who beat and killed him.

All over this earth, the Spirit of Jesus the Forgiver calls out to the lost. Thanks for praying with us that this particular son of Adam and many others will heed the call.

LAND OF DISCHARGE

The passing of time could be marked by the march of sunspots across the cracked cement floor. The sunspots existed thanks to bullet holes splashed across the tin roof. Unexceptional argument was reinforced by the distant rumble of artillery and the crackle of small-arms fire. Nearby in the cozy guesthouse, the garden was landscaped with bomb shelters and the wall stuccoed by shrapnel. Southern Sudan was the location for this General Assembly of churches, and I cannot remember a more exciting meeting.

The church here has been divided without amicability the last four years. Abuse of power, position and pennies has prevailed. This assembly (the first in four years) was called in order to bring some settlement to the animosity. The four-day meeting soared to the heights of blustery oratory and sunk to the level of shameful exposure. It fell apart several times, only to live again through urgent CPR.

In the end all 11 leaders who sat on the ruling council were discharged without honor. Some went meekly, others scratched and whined.

It was a sobering and emotionally exhausting assembly, yet it reinforced to me a basic truth. We are all accountable. If we do not accomplish our mandated purpose, what happened to the temple and the fig tree will certainly happen to us.

May we be faithful with the tasks, large and small, set before us. Please continue to pray for us that we will serve Sudan in the way we have been mandated from above. Please pray that we will discharge our duties faithfully, joyfully and enduringly.

LAND OF MIXED MESSAGES

Airports have always been a favorite haunt of mine. As I child, I would love to go to the Nairobi airport with my father when he would receive visitors. My first date with Jennifer was at an airport. I love the emotion latent in tearful farewells and joyous hellos. Other emotions also erupt sometimes.

An elderly couple recently arrived in Khartoum bringing with them several years' supply of condoms. The official at customs was a little confused. First, he did not know what they were and asked to open one. Second, he wanted to know why there were so many. The couple only had a one-month entry visa and the oversize Ziploc bag was full to the bursting. With a befuddled look, the official gazed at the 50-year-old couple, a huge bag of condoms and a one-month visa. His mental wheels were turning and he was not quite comfortable with his own conclusions.

Working among Muslims it is very easy to send mixed messages. We confuse Muslims by talking about morality and then dressing in short sleeves and short skirts. We confuse Muslims by endorsing the cheek-turning Jesus and then vigorously defending our right to bear arms. We confuse Muslims by denigrating their fusion of faith and politics then bemoan the lack of prayer in our public schools. We confuse Muslims when we claim to be a missionary and then spend the majority of our time fixing the car, visiting ex-patriots or blinking at the computer. We confuse Muslims when we invite them to a life that seems to be more chaotic and transient than their own. We confuse Muslims when we talk about peace but model impatience.

The longer we serve in the Muslim world, the more dependent we are on Jesus. False, frail and fleshly are we prone to be. In our own strength, we repel seeking hearts. What a wonder then that the precious Holy Spirit covers our failings and empowers us to represent Jesus well! This is perhaps to me the greatest miracle we see daily: Jesus flowing through clay pipes – pure, refreshing and life-giving.

Please continue to pray for us. Please pray that we would not sully the message of the cross. Please pray that the water of life flows through us, past us and over us, and directly into the hearts of so many Muslims who are so thirsty.

LAND OF GALLOPING GHOSTS

If you've been watching the news lately, I'm sure you are aware of the tragedy unfolding in Darfur, Western Sudan. We just returned from a trip there and were able to visit several refugee camps as we investigate how to best help the suffering.

Western Sudan is comprised of two basic collections of people. Arab Muslims and African Muslims. The Arab Muslims are pastoralists and the African Muslims are farmers. For centuries, times of drought have led to friction, as competition for limited water and arable land have increased. In the last two years, the competition became one-sided as the Sudanese government sided with the Arab Muslims. The result has been genocide: 2 million people displaced, hungry and at risk, over 140,000 slaughtered. The main aggressors are the so-called "jinjaweed" – a term that roughly translated means galloping ghosts. It refers to the Arab Muslim raiders who sweep into villages on horseback to kill and to plunder.

We arrived at the airport with sober excitement, only to find ourselves hemmed in by a padlocked gate. After five minutes of fiddling with several keys, the gatekeeper gave up and called in a supervisor. The supervisor was also thwarted in his efforts to release the grip of the padlock, and so with a shrug he walked over to the side of the gate and just lifted the whole gate off of its hinges. Then with a sweeping motion he grandly ushered us through.

Western Sudan is an area the size of Texas. It houses six million people, 99.99 percent Muslim. For years it has been nigh impossible to gain access to this area with the gospel. The region has remained locked despite our best fiddling. In one grand gesture, the current tragedy has been used to change all that. Jesus has in effect ignored the padlock and yanked the gate off of its hinges. A dozen Christian relief and development agencies have been able to access the region. Sudanese believers in cooperation with missionary teams are marching right in.

In a region long suppressed by galloping ghosts, the Holy Spirit has now been unleashed. He is himself quite the mover and shaker. Watch out devil, here comes [the] Calvary!

LAND OF RAMADAN

On the first day of Ramadan my fasting gave to me, a headache from the lack of fluids. (The traditional fast is abstinence from all food and water (including spit) from sunup to sundown.)

On the second day of Ramadan my feasting gave to me, two turtledoves for the fast breaking with neighbors in the street. (Ironically, more food is consumed during Ramadan than in any other month).

On the third day of Ramadan my society gave to me, three-hour afternoon naps, closed stores and inefficiency all around. (The city grinds slowly by day and hops by night.)

On the fourth day of Ramadan my friends did give to me, four calls to become a Muslim. (A spirit of religion descends at Ramadan. Muslims are more missionary. Interestingly, some become more open to the gospel, others much harder.)

On the fifth day of Ramadan my Jesus gave to me, FIVE GOLDEN OPPORTUNITIES TO WITNESS.

On the sixth day of Ramadan my observations gave to me, six chances to thank the Lord that we live under grace, not law.

On the seventh day of Ramadan I had to navigate the Ramadan Sundown 500. (To drive in Ramadan when buses, bicycles and bipeds are rushing home to break the fast, is to take your life into your own hands. An intense (no rules) rally is immediately followed by a ghost town effect.)

On the eighth day of Ramadan the maids of society are complaining. They are tired of making nightly feasts. (Women will labor all day long so that the men can march in and devour.)

On the ninth day of Ramadan the Lords of the Land are leaping in anger at each other. (The veneer of good will/religiosity has started to fade and tempers flare. Little fights and squabbles break out all over the city.)

On the 10th day of Ramadan the ladies see the end in sight, and in anticipation of the feast, begin to clean their house, prepare their pantry and even take time for a dance step or two.

On the 11th day of Ramadan the piping from the mosque is getting annoying. (The last ten days of Ramadan are considered to have extra merit. Some men will stay up all night chanting the Koran over the loudspeaker. The 27th night is called the night of power. It is the night when Muslims believe the Koran was originally revealed. Most Muslims will stay up all night praying, asking for guidance. It is a great night for an all-night prayer meeting for us...we pray that Jesus will reveal himself in dreams and visions on this night.)

On the 12th day of Ramadan the drumbeat of a billion hearts thumps out a rhythm of relief. Another Ramadan finished. Another feast to enjoy with families and friends. For us, it's one more year to celebrate being allowed to lift up Jesus among the Muslim community.

LAND OF SHORT CUTS

The Internet has been a great leveler in ministry to Muslims. In the past when Muslims came to Jesus and began to witness, they were silenced, expelled or killed. But how do you kill the Internet?

There is a wonderful chat room on the Web called "Pal-Talk." It is a no holds barred approach to evangelism. It is in Arabic and many of the contributors are Muslim background believers (MBBs). Voices that were once silenced are now unstoppable. Many Muslims are drawn to the site in anger since the content is very penetrating and direct.

An MBB responds to them in kind firmness: "I used to be just like you, but go look at this verse in the Koran. Go read this hadiith. Think through this issue. Compare if you can who Jesus is and what he has done." Individuals can be drawn into private chat rooms and evangelism goes forth. It is so encouraging to hear MBBs check in from around the world, publicizing their new allegiance to Jesus.

One of these MBBs was recently in our capital city. He went to a local Internet cafe and began to witness online. Questions and answers flew back and forth. At one point he leaned back to stretch and to his surprise noticed his text on the screen next to him. He was chatting (witnessing) to the Muslim one meter from his left elbow.

The message traveled thousands of miles of copper wire and electronic wave, and one arm length of the Spirit's shortcut. As a result of this MBB's Internet witness, four Sudanese Muslims

ONE

have come to Jesus this week. We will now start the discipling process face to face.

Thank God for His long arms and his immediate reach.

LAND OF NEWSPAPERS

Spread on my desk beside my laptop is today's Arabic newspaper. An advertisement nine inches high by 15 inches wide, sponsored by the "Department of Scholars of Sudan," bears this comforting title: LEGAL EDICT (Fatwa) ON THE COMPULSION TO DEFENSIVE JIHAD AND THE DUTY OF LIBERATING THE IRAQ FAMILY.

There are multiple references to Koranic verses sanctioning violence to unbelievers, and then the writing gently crescendos to a declaration that everyone is obligated to kill, assault, defame, attack, insult, kidnap or bite (plus many other un-Victorian urgings) the nearest American.

There is no way an advertisement this large and provocative could escape the notice of the censoring committee, and therefore there must be some level of sanction by the authorities.

I do not know if you tire of receiving alarming reports from Sudan. I sometimes tire of sending them. The situation in Darfur (West Sudan) is still on your screens (we head there again this weekend). The coalition in the south, which is negotiating for peace, is fragmenting. The believers in the North continue to hiccup their way to maturity. Sometimes it makes me want to write my own "fatwa" against bad news.

A Sudanese believer reminded me this week that one of the blessings of living in a fallen earth is that we are kept hungry for heaven. One day the trumpet will sound, the Lord shall return and the "No more tears, pain, night nor death" fatwa shall be enacted, and then it will be a pleasure to read the news again.

LAND OF DOOR BELLS

Sleigh bells, jingle bells, doorbells, 'tis the season for them all. Jennifer shared something with me last night and I asked her to put it on paper for you:

155

"I've been struggling this past week with my effectiveness here. Sudanese ladies love my teahouse, they love my cakes, they even love me, but they don't, won't, it seems, love my Lord. They don't want to know my Savior. As I was praying yesterday, I was crying out my pain and frustration: 'Where is the harvest? Where are the laborers?' I feel overwhelmed in a field where the grain seems, to me, to be dead on the stalk, not ripe unto harvest.

"I went grocery shopping at noon. Arriving back home, I noticed my neighbor had a lot of visiting family coming and going. I went to check it out and found that one of the brothers had come from abroad to visit. I greeted everyone in the room but one bustling woman in the background and went back home. Two minutes later my doorbell rings and it is the woman I failed to greet. She said to me, 'Hello, my name in Nuur. I talked to your husband at Mahmoud's funeral. I'm very interested in Christianity. I've visited the international church in town and I liked what the pastor had to say. Your husband is a pastor, isn't he? Could we talk sometime about Christianity?'

"My hope was saved by the bell."

As we approach Christmas, may we remember, "He comes to make his blessings known, FAR AS THE CURSE IS FOUND." The name "Nuur" means light. Please pray with us for Nuur and all Sudanese. Pray that this Christmas Jesus would ring her bell and that his light will shine into the darkness.

LAND OF GRINCHES

It is Christmas time again and our wayward Western tradition imagines a portly bearded gentleman struggling up and down chimneys with a sack of loot to distribute, while long, sticky-fingered Grinches scheme their Christmas drear. I heard yesterday the story of a Grinch gone good.

Jacob is a Dinka who leads the young people's ministry at our church. He is full of passion for Jesus and for Muslims. It was not always that way. As a young man, Jacob and his gang of Grinches would beat up the Muslim kids in their neighborhood and cause mischief at the local mosque.

During Friday prayers they would pretend to be Muslims. They would sneak in the mosque, wash and line up in the prayer row. After the first prostration when everybody was nose-pressed to the carpet, the young men would slip out of line and steal all the shoes. Scrambling to stow the shoes and sandals in sacks, they would dash out of the mosque and down to the river where they launched their sailing slippers into the deep. All the parishioners would then be forced to make a barefooted pilgrimage home.

One day the Grinching went bad and two large Muslim guards trapped the boys in the mosque. They leaped the low wall and sprinted for the river. Fully clothed they dove with the sacks into the water and swam for the other side. The Muslim guards shouted across the river to other farmers and the boys found themselves trapped. Not to be dismayed, they released their hostages into the swift current and followed them downstream and around the bend.

Years later the Lord changed Jacob from a shoe stealer to a soul saver. He recently went back to that very mosque and patched things up with the Imam. Today, Jacob delights in sharing the love of Jesus with Muslims.

I am thankful for Jesus this Christmas. He has come to a world of Grinches, of whom I am the Grinchiest, washed us, changed us and given us power to complete his mission. Joy to the world!

LAND OF PEACE

Last night we huddled around our neighbors' television set and watched in hushed silence as a permanent ceasefire was signed between the warring Sudanese parties.

The President, Vice President, Minister of Foreign Affairs and leader of the rebel movement all spoke with glowing faces. The Muslim president finished his speech by shouting, "Hallelujah, hallelujah, hallelujah! There is no God but God. There is no God but God." Both Christians and Muslims roared their approval.

A new day has dawned in Sudan.

Of course there will be setbacks, challenges and frustrations ahead. The issue in Darfur remains unsettled. Corruption and greed already lurk. Yet today we enjoy the moment. We are so thankful for all your prayers over the last years and plead with you for more. Before us lies the potential of many Muslims saved, but it will not happen without your prayer.

LAND OF HARVEST TEACHERS

We are so proud of our staff here at the Academy. Now in our third year, we have some amazing teachers. They are hard working, gifted educators. They love the children (Muslim and Christian), and they visit the Muslim families. There is only one problem. We do not have enough of them.

The Academy is an English medium primary school that serves several key functions:

1) It provides visas for missionaries/teachers.
2) It allows us to build relationships with Muslim families in the community (the majority of our students are Muslim).
3) It gives our own MKs (missionary kids) a place to go to school.

If you are an elementary teacher and would be willing to serve in Sudan for two to three years, please let me know. An Education degree is required and you will have to apply through the Assemblies of God World Missions program (Missionary Associate Department). We currently need teachers for all elementary classes.

Annually, the school will take care of your airfare, visas, registration, lodging and utilities. You will need to raise your living expenses (about $1000 per month in pledges and $5000 in cash). You will need to arrive in Sudan by August 1.

I love how Oswald Chambers describes Isaiah's response to God's call in Isaiah 6. Chambers teaches it was not a specific mandate, but a general plea. Isaiah volunteered.

If you are a teacher or know one to pass this on to, please hear our general plea. We desperately need you in Sudan at the Academy. Will you come? There is no better time to be serving in this great land of Sudan. "Christmas is coming, and Aslan is on the move!"

LAND OF NORMAL

Often we are asked, "Now what is it that you do exactly? What does a normal day look like?" Well, I am not sure if I am the best person to comment even superficially on normality, or at least that is what my no-holds-barred sister regularly informs me. She considers me on the daft side of median. But for sake of argument, this is what yesterday looked like:

5:30 a.m. Alarm goes off and "snooze" is hit.

5:35 a.m. Snooze 2

5:40 a.m. Stumble to the kitchen, put the kettle on. Set up the chairs for prayer meeting.

6:00-7:00 a.m. Team prayer meeting

7:00-7:15 a.m. Plan new ministry center in Darfur with partner agency

7:15-7:30 a.m. Dress boys for school; breakfast

7:30-7:45 a.m. Drive kids to school (narrowly avoiding several tickets while getting the giggling kids there by an unorthodox route)

7:45-8:00 a.m. Check on staff at the school

8:00-8:30 a.m. Answer email, read sports and news headlines on Internet, and wonder how I could get Roger Clemens to tithe to Sudan on his new salary of $18 million annual salary.

8:30-9:30 a.m. Quiet time

9:30-10:00 a.m. Pay bills

10:00-10:30 a.m. Pick up passport from Embassy for one of our staff traveling to a seminar

10:30-11:00 a.m. Meet with the Minister of Health to plan

upcoming hospital project

11:00-12:30 p.m. Meet with students in Islamics program for weekly mentoring session

12:30-2:30 p.m. Visit two hospital sites in preparation for medical project. Tell them "yes" on monitors, ventilators and sonograms, thanks to Assist International and Southern Cal. district, and "no" - we cannot refinance the national debt nor build all the doctors retirement homes.

2:30-2:45 p.m. Meet with two team members and solve issue

2:45-3:00 p.m. Meet with engineer and approve site for El Obeid Ministry center

3:00-4:00 p.m. Meet with two other team members, fail to solve their issue, small progress made

4:00-4:14 p.m. Jump on the trampoline with the boys (stranger walking by our gate does quadruple take on the "now you see me, now you don't" white man bobbing in and out of sight)

4:14-4:15 p.m. Pick my nose (the hot, dry climate is a picker's paradise)

4:15-4:20 p.m. Quick bite to eat (not related to above)

4:20-6:00 p.m. Work in office, preparing lessons for next week's seminar

6:00-6:30 p.m. Supper with South African partners who are staying with us for a week

6:30-7:30 p.m. Play outside with the boys

7:30-7:40 p.m. Put the boys down for the night

7:40-7:45 p.m. Meet with new missionary who borrows my drill and one DVD

7:45-8:15 p.m. Drive one of the South Africans to his appointment

8:15-10:15 p.m. House church meeting with Muslim background believers

10:30-11:00 p.m. Talk to Jenn

1:30 a.m. Wake up so I can take the South Africans to the airport

And there you have it. In the down time between the above, the cell phone rings repeatedly. I alternate between cursing it and answering it. Not all days are as busy as yesterday, but they all go just as quickly. We are so thankful to the Lord to be in Sudan at this time.

LAND OF BROKEN DOORS

I guess sometimes Jesus gets tired of knocking gently. If you thumb through Patrick Johnstone's Operation World 2004 edition, you will notice that he lists three places as "the most unreached on earth." They are: Western Sudan / Eastern Chad (Darfur area), the Afghanistan/Pakistan/Iran confluence and the island of Sumatra, Indonesia.

In the last few years (Afghanistan in 2003, Darfur in 2004, Indonesia in 2004-05), all three of these areas have been knocked down by tragedy and one of the results has been astonishing access by Christians (relief, development, missions).

How interesting that the three most inaccessible places on earth have had their doors bashed in by the gentle knuckles of Jesus. How fiercely he loves this world. What a terrifyingly wonderful day we live in.

As a family working in one of the above areas, we see only one hitch in the plan: Not enough people to walk through the knocked-down doors. The financial response has been generous and the opportunities are incredible; so where are the laborers? If Jesus is gently knocking on the door of your missions heart, it probably would be a good moment to respond. He can sometimes knock rather forcefully.

LAND OF IDENTITY

Third culture kids move around so much, they are not always sure where to call home, and when they're ankle biters, even their geography is suspect. Zack prayed the other night, "Lord, help us to preach the gospel everywhere they speak English, except hell." Luke came home from his karate lesson, dramatically dividing the air into quadrants and then yelling, "Ayeeeeeeeeee Akbar!"

When Jennifer lifted her eyebrows, he explained, "Oh, that is just the God of Karate." It takes a third culture kid to combine martial arts and the Muslim creed.

A woman in Sudan recently gave her heart to the Lord. She stopped going to the mosque with her family and she stopped the ritual prayers five times daily. When questioned she simply replied, "I have found Someone who means all the world to me!" Her father flew into a rage, beat her severely and tried to gouge her eyes out. "You have become one of THEM!" he screamed and took up a pair of scissors to stab her. Her brother lunged for the father's arm and Mt. Moriah-like stopped its dreadful descent. Instead of a stabbing, this beautiful saint had all her hair roughly chopped off and was expelled from the house.

It is wonderfully painful for Sudanese who change identities. Becoming a child of God in this context includes suffering. Please pray for "Fatima" as she identifies with Jesus. Pray that she can somehow show his love to those who are so hurt by her transition.

LAND OF BOOTLEGGING

When my name has made the newspapers, it has not always been for the best of reasons. When a teenager, the local Kenyan pastor in the village where we lived arrived breathless at my father's door with a story about my buddies and I jumping off a 100-foot bridge into the Indian Ocean. Parents do not usually like to find out their kids summer activities from the "National Daily."

Today was another one of those black ribbon days. The outside page of the largest Arabic newspaper accuses us of running an illegal alcohol distribution ring from our Ladies Community Center. Again, not exactly what your parents want to read about you.

Yesterday, we discovered that the watchman at the Ladies Center had hidden a box of imported alcohol on the premises. We immediately told him to "whiskey" it away, and while he did we searched his room. We found 12 cases (12 one-liter bottles in each case) of vodka, Jack Daniels and their friends. We immediately called the police and they stationed a detective in the guard's room. When he returned, he was arrested along with his accomplice.

The friendly police chief, a charming chap, insisted we were involved, and the lovely article in the paper today charges the same thing.

We have worked very hard to build the Ladies Community Center into a place where Muslim women feel safe. The devil is obviously trying to undermine our credibility with one false stroke. The police are threatening to close down the center.

Please pray with us that Jesus (as he has done for us so many times before) will give the devil the boot and force his legions to leg it out of here. Pray that a "prohibition of The Spirit" will protect us from all attacks of the enemy. Pray that the Center will stay open and that many Muslim ladies would be able to taste the new wine therein.

LAND OF FAMILY

"Matthew" continues to grow in faith. Last week he was kicked out of the local mosque for talking about Jesus incessantly. A big burly bearded bear threatened physical violence if he came back to the mosque to talk about the Christ. Matthew, still needing accompanying growth in sanctification, threatened right back saying, if he saw this man in the street, he would in like manner not allow him passage.

If you do not tell anyone, I will admit that I am proud of my brother. Not because he still has a temper but because he has the courage to stand up against opposition.

In a more subdued tone yesterday, Matthew shared the pain he feels as a result of family rejection. His brother has not spoken one word to him in two years even though they live in the same house. If Matthew is in the sitting room with family friends and his brother enters, the brother will greet and shake hands with everyone in the room, skipping over Matthew entirely as if he did not even exist.

It helped put my relational disappointments in perspective. "I am so glad that I'm a part of the family of God." Thank you for being our extended family. Thanks for talking to us, and more so for talking to the Father for us. In your next family conversation, please hold up Matthew as well.

LAND OF SPITTLE AND SPEED

One hundred-eighty kilometers per hour (not one km per hour exaggeration) is fast at any speed; let alone when you are at the mercy of a driver who was mentored by a butterfly. Zipping and dipping, swerving unnerving, we flew down the desert road. The fancy Toyota we were in had a helpful little beeping warning whenever the speedometer dared to slip past 120. As we were pretty much always on the right side of 160, you can pretty much drop the "p" from the word "helpful."

Our destination was a little village school and dedication ceremony. Various ones of you gave funds to provide clean water to the whole village and four new classrooms for the all-girls school. Each class will host 65 girls. Each class is about 150-square feet. The Minister of Education is a friend of ours and it was his driver assigned to help improve my prayer life. The national press was present and so I tried very hard not to pick my nose on camera.

After the facility inspection the minister presented several other gifts to the community (Malaria prevention, orphan aid, school desks) and launched into his political speech. I listened intently to him with my left ear, while my right was overpowered by the screaming fundamentalist who, without pause, shouted out such encouragement as "the whole world will be Muslim" and "the Koran is our only constitution." As we were sitting in a football ground, he was also kind enough to remind us that the players had on the uniforms of colonialists and they should don the Muslim robe before continuing to play. The poor man really worked himself into a sweat; I am sure he will sleep well tonight.

Or maybe he won't. Maybe gentle Jesus heard quite enough nonsense for one day. Maybe the seeker Shepherd's concern for those speeding and spitting their way to eternity will manifest in a dream or a personal appearance. To minister, motorist and maniac, "Come, Lord Jesus, come!"

PART ONE

LAND OF BURNING

"Darfur Debbie" was sitting by her family's orchard when the horse-backed bandit rode up with a jerry can of petrol. He calmly doused all of the fruit trees, clambered up on his horse and threw a match over his shoulder. That was almost two years ago. Since then Debbie has come to Jesus.

Debbie was standing on the side of the dusty road in town with her sisters when a taxi slowed and stopped. As she bent to negotiate the fare, she recognized the driver as the same bandit who had so callously destroyed her family's primary source of food and wealth.

Her sisters refused to get in but Debbie calmly climbed aboard, greeted the man and let him drive her home. He was so astonished that he refused to take any payment.

Debbie testifies, "Before I came to Jesus, I could only think of revenge but now I feel only peace and love, even towards him."

The good news about Darfur is the Good News. Debbie led her husband and her brother to the Lord. Her brother prayed for an elderly blind man who was instantly healed. The blind man sent 11 other men to Debbie and her brother to hear the gospel. They came to Jesus and returned to their war ravaged area and are meeting twice a week with Christ as their center.

So the next time you hear the gruesome statistics from Darfur – the ladies raped, the children killed, the villages scorched – please remember that there is another fire burning. A holy one. A cleansing flame. And this fire is very hard to douse, very hard indeed.

LAND OF REFORMATION

It is not every day that you get to preach to Martin Luther. The new commander of all forces in Darfur (26,000 peacekeeping troops from both The African Union and the United Nations) is a Nigerian general of that name. Last weekend I was invited to address the Christian troops in Darfur – with General Martin Luther in attendance. I shelved the "indulgences" sermon and cast about for something on grace.

These God-fearing troops are amazing. Not only have they started a Christian Fellowship for the soldiers, they have also bought land by a refugee camp, built a school, opened a church on the property and will shortly add a clinic ALL on their own time and with their own finances. Additionally, they are great escorts. After the Saturday evening service they drove us back to our center in convoy. Two armored vehicles and two pick-ups, one of which had a heavy caliber machine gun mounted on the back. It kind of made me wish the Jinjaweed would attack. What could be more effective than a bunch of prayed up West Africans with big guns?

Almost weekly the testimonies trickle out of Darfur. A Muslim background believer (MBB) received a message from other secret believers in Khartoum: "We are sending you a box of biscuits. Please pick them up at the bus depot." She scurried down to the station and found the box of "biscuits" to be unusually heavy. The Word of God is weighty indeed.

There are reports of group conversion. There is the reality of a village of former Muslims erecting their own church building. There are the repeated whispers of Sheikhs coming to Jesus. A reformed Darfur. Luther would be proud. I am sure his Lord is elated.

LAND OF OSAMA BIN-CHRISTMAS

I just flew in this weekend from the main Sudanese port. Located on the Red Sea this port city is the closest city to Mecca outside of Saudi Arabia – just over 200 miles away. It is a city and a region deeply bound and oppressively dark. A colleague and I were visiting in order to re-open our English education center.

The airport in this city was built by Osama Bin Ladin during his sojourn here in Sudan in the early 1990s. It is clean, air-conditioned, spacious and decked out with flat screen high definition televisions. As we waited for our plane, I was amused by the music being pumped into the terminal by the public sound system. "I'm dreaaaaaaming of a whiiiite

Christmas!" was promptly followed by "Jesus, Lord at thy

birth." Some dear soul availed himself of a Christmas album. Osama must be turning over in his cave.

As we stood in the bus that ferried us from the airplane to the terminal, the cell phone of the Muslim man next to me rang. It was a Scottish bagpipe rendition of "Amazing Grace."

Despite the best efforts of Osa-mice and men, the gospel message penetrates. The music above meant little to the Muslims hearing it but to me it was a pertinent reminder: "If we descend to the very pit of hell, Jesus is there." What an honor it is to bring the light and music of Christ to the darkest places on earth. Your prayers linked to our actions help us broadcast in stereo. I think it is time to crank up the volume.

LAND OF TOE PULLING

I am learning that some of the best appointments are initially the least welcome. Last night at 9:30, I was just starting to close the chapter on a busy day by opening up the wit of P.G. Woodhouse. I was settling down in my bed to read when the phone rang. The friendly neighborhood sheikh insisted I come over to his house.

I threw on my Jalabiya and shuffled down the dirty road muttering to myself, angry that I had answered the phone. I fostered a fake smile, stepped into the sheikh's compound and was immediately introduced to a member of the royal family of Qatar. The prince had made himself at home in the courtyard, splashing carpets and cushions around in regal style. Servants were cooking the ducks they had shot that morning and I was invited to lounge on some cushions next to the prince.

As we reclined, enjoying the wafted scent of the cooking ducks, we talked about politics, hunting and religion. At one point in the midst of our conversation, the sheikh grabbed my foot and began cracking the knuckles on my toes by viciously pulling each one. "Thanks" was as eloquent a reply as I could muster in my surprise.

A feast was served, prayers were offered and then we settled back on the cushions to talk. It turned out that I had been summoned to give the prince hunting advice for his upcoming trip to

Kenya. Now I readily admit to being as capable as the next male of squashing the odd cockroach now and then, but falconry and hounds are above my pay grade. The conversation thus returned to spiritual things.

At about 1 a.m., I was able to share the gospel simply and clearly with the Qatari prince. He listened quietly and respectfully and soon I was on my way home; the Sheikh my escort. Two men from different worlds, serving different kings, hand-in-hand down the moonlit road. I quietly hoped he would not start yanking on my fingers.

And so the chase is on, a royal hunter not yet cognizant that the Hound of Heaven has picked up the scent. The one who loses none will pull on their hearts, not just their toes.

LAND OF THE JINJAWEED

It was a normal trip to Darfur. Same old boring stuff: refugee camps, checkpoints, project inspections, an old brown Land Rover (filled with machine gun-toting government soldiers) with a Nike swoosh emblazoned on its door and a "meet-and-greet" with the Jinjaweed.

The pastor of our partner church in Nyala (South Darfur) picked me up Sunday morning and asked me to preach. The church is made up of immigrant Dinka (Southern Sudanese) who migrated to this completely Muslim province looking for work. I had been avoiding the pastor as I knew he would want me to preach and I was neither prayed up nor prepared.

As the congregants sang I racked my brain trying to remember what I had just shared with the Khartoum team from Revelation 2 concerning the persecuted church of Smyrna. Rather pleased with myself for remembering most of the details, I began to pontificate on the Age of the Martyrs, Polycarp and the 10 declarations of persecution issued by the Roman emperors of the first two centuries AD. The pastoralist Dinka showed their great enthusiasm for the topic and my articulate presentation style by taking a group nap. I think I would of gotten along better if I had addressed urinary tract infections in one-horned

168

nomadic cows, though finding supporting texts would have been problematic.

Just as I reached the verse "Do not fear..." and began to encourage the believers not to be intimidated by Islam, the Lord allowed a fitting illustration. A group of almost 200 Jinjaweed rode up to and then directly passed the humble church. They were mounted on camels and horses, heavily armed with machine guns and spears. They were dirty, disheveled and intimidating. It took them several minutes to file by. Outside in the village, people scattered in all directions while inside the pastor calmly gave instructions for the children to be held by their parents. It did not do much for the pastor's nerves but greatly helped his "first time visitor' statistics. This was the morning after the massacre at the African Union camp, a day's ride to the east, and the Jinjaweed were coming from that very direction.

One of the most gripping aspects of God's heart is his complete devotion to all peoples of the earth. His love and passion for the Jinjaweed is no less than for you or I. Jesus holds out his blood-stained arms to these killers, rapists and baby brutalizers. His love for the violent runs as deep as his gentle care for the victims. I wonder how many of God's people around the world have ever had this Romans 9:2-3 thought cross their mind: "I have great sorrow and continual grief in my heart. For I could wish that I myself were accursed from Christ for my brethren, my Jinjaweed, according to the flesh."

"For God so loved the Jinjaweed..."

LAND OF THANKS

On Tuesday I received a call from a MBB (Muslim background believer). He made a profession of faith in Jesus almost 10 years ago and has walked wobbly ever since. We have continually helped him through the years, in times of crisis, only to have him disappear until such a time as he needs more money. The call informed us that his child was sick and that he needed immediate assistance. Having been down this road many times before, I immediately prayed about what to do and felt a leading to ask this man to trust Jesus in this situation and not me. He sent me a text, "By God I will never leave you [I will hunt you] and your organization and every thing you have a relationship with if my daughter is dead!"

On Wednesday I got an urgent call from the wife of another MBB. She is not a believer but knows he is and she was crying on the phone. "Come quickly!" she begged. I jumped in the car and raced to their house to find them in the midst of a violent and terrible domestic dispute. She had been beaten and her face was badly swollen. For the next two hours, I did my best Darfur peacekeeper impersonation as two infuriated people yelled at each other in Arabic.

Today is Thanksgiving and the threats and screams of this week remind me of how crucial it is to "give thanks in all things, for this is the will of God." We should give "thanks for pain, and thanks for pleasure," according to hymn writer August Ludvig Storm. So buckle your seat belts. Here goes:

I am thankful for MBBs who threaten me and who shout at each other, for it reminds me that at least there are MBBs.

I am thankful for liberals, for they remind me that sometimes it is better to be soft-hearted and wrong than hard-hearted and right.

I am thankful for the Koran, for it reminds me how much I love reading the Bible.

I am thankful for the violent tragedy of Darfur, for it is driving many into the arms of Jesus.

I am thankful for radical Muslims, for they are one of the best arguments for Christ.

I am thankful that the leading Republican candidates are pro-choice, for it forces the people of God to look at additional issues.

I am thankful for persecution and poverty, for it helps the church to be radical, simple and vibrant.

I am thankful for global warming talk, for if a little temperature lift has the world concerned, then perhaps the fires of hell will become a more widely recognized "inconvenient truth."

I am thankful for hunger, for it reminds me where my real food comes from and that it is the will of God not the swill of man.

I am thankful for bigotry, because it illuminates the prejudice in my own heart and illumination is half the battle.

I am thankful for potholes, for they remind me of a city with streets of gold where no driver dare turn left across four lanes of speeding angels.

I am thankful for my failures, for they remind me that there is a God and I am not him.

I am thankful for sand, dust, thirst, heat and prayer calls, for they increase my appreciation for fir trees and still cool waters.

I am thankful for expulsion and exclusion, for they remind me the Kingdom gates are wide open.

I am thankful for the devil and his demons, for they remind me that many more angels surround us and that their vileness merely accents the goodness of God.

I am thankful that life is hard, for it helps me release it and reach for home. And home, after all, is where Thanksgiving is best celebrated.

LAND OF RABBITS

I am told that rabbits reproduce themselves quickly. As a lover of missiology and with the current attention on Church Planting Movements (CPMs), I thought that the purchase of bunnies for my animal-loving son Zack might help me understand the process of rapid reproduction.

I did indeed learn one very important lesson. Unless you are a microscopic cell, a calculator or a "Rocky" movie, it's tough to multiply all by yourself.

Occasionally, we let the bunnies out to scamper and on one of these occasions we could not find Peter Rabbit. We searched high and low to no avail. Three days passed. Our first whiff of Peter was not a pleasant one. I opened the hood of the car to find his fried little body wedged between the battery and the chassis. Though the car is a hatchback Volkswagen, I am not sure that this is what the designers had in mind. I removed the PETA bumper sticker.

Peter Rabbit had been to town, school, the bank, the airport, the market and to numerous homes in between over the last few days, but obviously did not get to enjoy the journey. And needless to say Petunia Rabbit is not going to be doing any multiplying in the near future.

I want to ask specific prayer for three MBB men, none of which have believing wives. All three of these men have shown tremendous growth in Christ the past few years. Their wives continue to resist the gospel and in so doing have made it very hard for the men to raise the children (15 from the three families) in a biblical manner.

Please pray for our three Petunias. It is unified MBB couples that have the "together strength" needed for growth in this harsh context.

LAND OF SPANKINGS

Friends of ours recently moved to a new house in an all-Muslim neighborhood.

A mother and son live above them. The husband/father has been absent for five years due to his work in England. The little 5-year-old rascal was an unholy terror, disobedient, kicking, shouting and abusive to his mother. The mother is interested in the gospel: reading the Bible consistently, sometimes spending several hours of the day visiting and watching with wonder the well-behaved missionary kids.

On one recent visit the little hot head went into his tantrum routine. Our friend asked the mother if he could discipline her son. Shocked, she agreed. The little boy was talked to sternly but he reacted rudely. So our friend turned him over his knee and spanked him. The boy was told to apologize to his mother. He ran to his mother and grabbed her leg but refused to apologize. So our friend turned him over his knee and spanked him again.

The spanking has worked wonders. The behavior of the boy has completely changed. He is now a little angel. The mother is ecstatic and one large bound closer to the Kingdom.

Now in most books and seminars, spanking the children of neighbors you are trying to reach with the love of Christ does not get prime advocacy. Last I checked it has not climbed into the list of "Top 10 Ways to Share Your Faith With Muslims." How ironic that what could get you thrown in jail in Sweden is used by the Spirit in Sudan to bring a broken family to healing and hope.

The longer I am in the Muslim world, the more skeptical I am of the latest methodology and frantic search for the "golden key" that will open the door to mass conversions. It all comes down to the simple and faithful repetition of three encounters: Love, Truth and Power.

We must love Muslims – sharing life with them one-on-one, life-on-life, with all its joys and sorrows, all its peaks and valleys.

We must truth Muslims – inviting them to bible study and spending extended time in the Word of God with them.

We must power Muslims – praying for the signs, wonders, miracles, dreams and power encounters of the Spirit to confirm the still small voice that calls out to them in mercy.

When these three encounters are our bedrock, then anything, even spankings, can be the strategy of the Spirit. Now, if I can only figure out how to evangelistically use bacon and eggnog.

LAND OF PRO-CHOICE

Thomas walked out of church as a taxi with three Arab Muslims squealed to a stop. The taxi contained three Muslims, two men and a woman, and the woman was writhing under the control of demons. The men told Thomas, "We are bringing her to church as we do not know what to do!"

Thomas brought the lady inside the church and began with others to rebuke the evil spirits. For over an hour they prayed for the lady as her friends watched curiously from the side. After an hour of praying in the Spirit, the spirits were cast out and the woman freed.

Thomas walked over to the Arab Muslim men and said, "What you just witnessed is the power of Jesus." Awed at answered prayer, one of the men said, "My daughter is in the hospital for a serious operation. Can you please pray for her?"

The next Sunday the man came back to church beaming/ He sat through the service and stood to testify. "Your prayers worked! The operation for my daughter was perfectly successful! Please pray that same prayer again. She has another operation coming up shortly."

The Muslim man returned to his seat, but Thomas rose from his and pulled the man outside. "You are experiencing the power of Jesus, but that is not enough! You need to repent of your sins and make Jesus Lord and Savior and you need to do it now. Today is your day for salvation."

The Arab Muslim man bowed his head, repented of sin and invited Jesus into his heart. He now meets Thomas regularly for discipleship and bible study.

All over this world, Muslims are making decisions to follow Jesus. Let us not be reluctant to present them with the opportunity. Let's be pro-choice. Many will choose life.

LAND OF UNBELIEF

Three weeks ago Ahmad gave his life to Jesus. A devout Muslim who prayed five times a day, he is radically saved. His uncle is a Sheikh who always begins his prayers with "Bismillah Ar-Rahman Ar-Rahiiiiiiiiiiiiiiim" (In the name of God most merciful, most Compassionate). Ahmad responds to him: "I thank Jesus for everythiiiiiiiiiiiiiiiing." Ahmad is a student at our English center.

Two weeks ago Jasmin gave her life to Jesus. Unsure of what it means for her safety and future, she counted it more precious to believe in Jesus and walk with him then to stay safe and spiritually lost. Jasmin is a teacher at one of our schools.

A week ago Mahmoud gave his life to Jesus. A street vendor who had grown disenchanted with Islam, he entered bible study and opened his heart to the Savior. Ahmad, newly saved and full of fire, helped welcome Mahmoud into the family.

Two days ago, Safa gave her life to Jesus. She was led to the Lord by her brother-in-law (himself a convert from Islam and the director of another of our English centers) and they now have plans to start a small house church.

In the last month a government minister has come to Christ. She watched a video about Jesus and that was enough for her. She has already been baptized. She is showing that same video to all the friends and family that she can.

In the last month a woman had a dream of Jesus dressed in traditional Sudanese clothing. He was shining white and invited her to follow him. "But I am a Muslim!" she protested. He led her to a clear stream and poured three cups of water over her head. Confused she later asked her Muslim taxi driver what it meant. "You need to ask a Pastor," he replied. She found a pastor and was led to Jesus.

In the last month I know of five other Muslims who have given their life to Jesus.

In 12 years in Sudan we have never seen anything like this. It is unbelievable. We have just finished a season of prayer and fasting. People all over the world are praying for Sudan. Whatever Sudan was, something has broken. It can no longer be called a land of unbelief.

LAND OF COMMAND

Late one night last week, one our Sudanese staff was driving home. He unwittingly drove by the home of a militia commander. A soldier jumped in front of him with rifle raised. He swerved to miss him only to hit another armed soldier. Dragged out of the car, he was beaten, arrested and came within a hair of being executed. Another two of our staff went to negotiate his release and were in turn arrested and threatened. Unless they brought the legal papers of the car and surrendered them as a "gift" to the commander and the paltry sum of $250,000 by 2 p.m. the next day, they would be eliminated.

The long running wars of Sudan have bred "commanders" who are laws unto themselves. This particular one is actually from southern Sudan, but quarreled with his superior and subsequently fled to the North where he now performs the dirty work of the regime. When rebels attached Omdurman (the western part of the capital city Khartoum) last month, it was this commander and his militia that repulsed them. He is accountable to no one. He has his own prison, his own security police and his own militia. His word is law and everyone is afraid of him.

I was sitting at my desk when our staff member walked in at 12:30 p.m. He was in obvious shock and despair. We had an hour and a half to find the legal papers of the car and a bundle of money. If we failed to respond, we feared for the life our colleague still in militia custody. These soldiers are uneducated and ruthless. They have been killers for two decades and life (at least that of others) is just to be wasted. Fear spread its palpable fingers out and reached for our hearts. Life seems so fleeting when you are staring down the barrel of a gun held angrily by unprincipled men.

Unless you have live in a land or through a situation where the forces of evil are accountable to no earthly power, it is difficult to understand the feelings of anger and hopelessness that invade your spirit. All of us, in our flesh, having nowhere to run, wanted to go find a gun and take the militia on. I can see how violence begets violence. Instead we fired off prayers. They fly truer than bullets.

By miracle the staff member escaped the militia and we decided not to give into their demands and hid the staff in a safe house. We approached some influential leaders who bravely agreed to approach the commander to request the return of our vehicle. After much tension the vehicle was released to us and the $250,000 fee was reduced to $5,000 for damages done to the soldier (broken leg). They are still threatening our staff (they stole their money, phones and national ID cards, which gave details of residence) and so our staff is still in hiding.

After a couple tense days I have added to my mental list of courses they do not cover in university: "How to outmaneuver terrorist commanders." It probably should not be a freshman level course.

God is in control, even when life isn't. There really is not a blessed thing that we can do to ensure the ongoing safety of our staff. These militia are so vengeful and irrational, their security apparatus so detailed and cunning, that at anytime in the future they could hunt our staff and/or families down. We are in a situation that is not controlled and cannot be contained. It is an open-ended menace. And we are perfectly safe.

"No guilt in life, no fear in death,
This is the power of Christ in me.
From life's first cry to final breath,
Jesus commands my destiny.
No power of hell, no scheme of man
Can ever pluck me from his hand.
Till he returns or calls me home,
Here in the power of Christ I'll stand."
— "In Christ Alone" by Keith Getty and Stuart Townend

Rejoice with us that Jesus is the Commander of Angel Armies. He is Lord of Hosts. We are under his authority, his protection and his command. Jesus commands our destiny.

LAND OF WASTE

It would be interesting to log the hours Muslims spend in prayer. Sudan has over 40 million people. Seventy percent of Sudan is Muslim. Allowing for that percentage, children and non-practicing Muslims, let us say that 10,000,000 people pray five times a day in the Sudan. If each prayer period lasts five minutes, that totals 250,000,000 minutes (4,166,000 hours or 173,611 days or 475 years) of futile prayer a day. Think of it. Every day in Sudan there is a cumulative 475 years of wasted prayer!

By contrast, if you would like to pray to the living God on behalf of this nation and her beautiful sons and daughters, the time spent approaching the Father for the issues below will not be wasted.

1) Pray for wide proclamation. The tendency in missions and the pressure in a Muslim context is to concentrate on some kind of humanitarian assistance and then only share the gospel at rare times. Please pray that missionaries and Christian workers in Sudan would be gripped

with a renewed fire to always share the gospel. Pray that we would feel like Jeremiah: "fire shut up in our bones" if we do not proclaim.

2) Pray for MBBs to be baptized in the Holy Spirit. There are a lot of half truths, half commitments, half standing for Christ. Full, bold steps are not taken because of fear. Pray that there would be an infilling of Holy Spirit power so that MBBs would stand up in faith, bear the consequences, become stronger and witness further.

3) Pray for laborers to be thrust into the harvest field. Pray for strategic cities like Port Sudan, Atbarra, Shendi and El Obeid that have very little missionary presence and great darkness. Pray for the Arab tribes of Sudan, which are largely unreached with the gospel. Specifically pray for the Shagiyya and Jaaliya, the two dominant Arab peoples of Sudan.

4) Pray for Darfur. War and suffering have brought so many to Jesus. Please pray that the war and injustice will NOT STOP UNTIL GOD'S PURPOSE IS ACCOMPLISHED. I know this sounds like a strange request. But strategically it is suffering that has made Muslims in Darfur turn to Jesus.

5) Pray for a unity of spirit among MBB leaders. Pray that we would be able to have consistent meetings with them, so that they can establish trust and in the future partner together in the love of Christ. Pray for key MBB leaders to emerge who would be catalysts for unity and leadership among other MBBs.

6) Pray that the Word of God would rise. Through song, through media, through video, through literature, through journalism, through satellite, through cassette and radio, through the voices and words of God's people, pray that

Scripture is widely disseminated and goes everywhere, into every ear. Pray that there is a hunger for the word of the Lord.

7) Pray for protection from the darts and schemes of the roaring lion who would seek to devour missionaries, MBBs and southern Christians. Pray against discouragement. Pray against the darts of delayed visas and corrupt systems. Pray against gossip, conflict in teams and competition between teams. Pray against demonic activity and oppression. Pray against confusion and bad decisions. Pray against lies and bondages.

8) Pray for the opportunity to pray with (not just for) influential leaders in government and society. Pray for access to the influencers. Pray that leaders of government, military, industry, education and false religion come running to Jesus and as "Men of Peace" influence others.

LAND OF WHISTLES

If you scrolled carefully down the list of Olympic nations, you will have noticed that the Sudan earned one silver medal. The tally would have been a more commendable gold and silver had not the organizing committee given in to the pressure to ban plastic whistling.

Sudanese are the champions of these infernal insults and Sudanese policemen are the whoppers of whistling.

The typical Sudanese policeman stands in the middle of chaotic intersections and cheerfully puffs on his plastic. His arms wave randomly and he blows furiously as if he was a woman in labor. Sudan being what it is, by 11 a.m. it is well over 100 degrees, yet our Olympic whistlers are undeterred. The arms stop moving but the cheeks keep puffing and shrill bursts randomly stream out in undecipherable patterns.

By 1 p.m. it has nosed up to 120 degrees in the intersection sun, so our whistlers, also being wise, saunter over to the corner and find the nearest shade – be it umbrella, overhang or Palm tree – and keep whistling. Their arms might have betrayed them. They might even lean back and rest their weary eyes, but their lips do not flag nor fail. They just sit in the shade blasting the pernicious plastic while traffic snarls and comes to a complete stop. Even then the shrilling continues.

It all makes me wonder what my voice sounds like to the community that surrounds me. Am I shrill? Am I annoying? Do I help anyone or do I just sit out of the mess shouting impractical solutions? Am I in the middle of everything adding confusion?

The gospel is by nature a stumbling block to both Muslim and modern minds. May the Lord help us not to add unnecessary shrilling. Lets leave the empty gonging to others. May our voice be sweet, even if our message is troubling.

LAND OF CHEEKS

Sitting in my house recently, I was amused to hear the sincere question of a MBB. This man has gone through several years of persecution, trouble and rejection. He even had his family forcibly taken from him. Having had his natural fill, he wrinkled up his brow, spread his hands out palms up and asked, "When is it our turn to persecute them?"

A few weeks later I sat in a meeting listening in wonder to another MBB. His 26-year-old son, a university graduate, was butchered. His throat was slit by the angry Muslims of the family that he was trying to reach out to in the love of Jesus. This bereaved father, his eyes sparkling with love and grace for the ones who slaughtered his own son, said simply, "No cost is too great for the gospel."

How difficult it is to turn cheeks; we would much rather sit on them. How humbling it is to sit in the presence of men and women who have lost what is most precious, to see them struggle, and then to see them rise above their pain and shine. When they count it all joy to be pierced to the heart, it gives perspective to my complaints.

I am not unaware of the difficulty of the times. The American church has long been generous. For many our giving has been out of surplus disposable income. The majority of the world has long been giving out of sacrifice. We have the opportunity before us now to follow their lead.

Will we follow that lead with our children? Having absorbed the financial blow of raising and educating our precious own, will we know submit also to the emotional blow and relational toll of blessing them as they brave the slap of unreached peoples? Or is that cost too great for the gospel?

Keith Green said it well:

"Well I pledge my son, I pledge my wife.
I pledge my head to heaven.
I pledge my son, I pledge my wife.
I pledge my head to heaven...for the gospel."
— "Pledge My Head to Heaven" by Keith Green

Part Two

CHRIST-CENTERED COMMUNITIES IN THE SUDANESE MUSLIM CONTEXT

A study on the varied approaches

Christ-Centered Communities in a Muslim Context (The C1-C6 Spectrum)

Case Study: Sudan

John Travis is the architect of the C1-C6 spectrum. This spectrum represents the different forms of Christ-centered communities in Muslim lands and contexts. There is an entire journal devoted to these ideas and it is extremely helpful reading (*International Journal of Frontier Missions*, Vol. 17:1 Spring 2000). I will simply copy the chart and then analyze it in the Sudanese context, cross-referencing it to Joshua Massey's M1-M9 spectrum: Muslim attitudes about Islam.

The C1-C6 Spectrum

	C1	C2	C3	C4	C5	C6
CHRIST-CENTERED COMMUNITY DESCRIPTION	A church foreign to the Muslim community both in culture and language	Like C1, but speaking the language used by Muslims, though their religious terminology is distinctly non-Muslim	Like C2, but using non – Islamic cultural elements (e.g. dress, music, diet and arts)	Like C3, but with some Biblically acceptable Islamic practices	Like C4 with a "Muslim follower of Jesus" self identity	Secret believers, may or may not be active in the religious life of the community
SELF IDENTITY	"Christian"	"Christian"	"Christian"	"Follower of Isa"	"Muslim follower of Isa"	Privately "follower of Isa," or "Muslim Follower of Isa"
MUSLIM PERCEPTION	Christian	Christian	Christian	A kind of Christian	A strange kind of Muslim	Muslim

SUDAN CONTEXT

C1: Khartoum International Church is an example of the C1 model. The service is entirely conducted in English. The majority of the members are expatriates and missionaries. A few Christian background Sudanese attend. The church members would consistently identify themselves as Christians and are considered Christians by the community.

C2: Khartoum Christian Center is an example of the C2 model. This church belongs to the Sudan Pentecostal Church (SPC) and is conducted in Arabic. The level of Arabic is medium low since the members are southern Sudanese who grew up in the North and attended Arabic schools. While the members read and write standard Arabic, they tend to converse and sing in Juba (simplified) Arabic. They identify themselves as Christian and are perceived as Christians by the Muslim community.

C3: Bahri Evangelical Church is an example of the C3 model. This church is an independent church that was released from the mainline Presbyterian fellowship because it was quite active in evangelism and the spiritual gifts. Coptics who were born again founded the church. The level of Arabic is high, a few of the female members wear the traditional tobe (one piece of four-meter long material that wraps all the way around the ladies body for modesty), a few men wear the jellabiya (white Arab garment) and the style of music is closer to northern Sudanese ethnic music. This church still identifies itself as Christian and is perceived by Muslims as being Christian.

C4: "The Group" is a collection of two missionaries, one local Arab pastor and three Muslim Background Believers (MBBs). The group meets in a house, often wears the culturally northern attire, adopts some Islamic[1] forms of prayer and fasts Ramadan (though not always strictly in the Islamic fashion). When asked if they are Christians, they will reply with some sort of confession of allegiance to Jesus: "I am a follower of Isa" or "I have submitted myself and my life to God in Jesus the Christ," but they will not claim to be a Muslim. They are still perceived, however, to be Christians (especially the missionaries), albeit strange ones.

C5: There is a family of Muslims who came to Christ as the result of their patriarchs' dreams of Jesus. They meet together in homes and even now there are second generation MBBs (if such an anomaly is possible). They are similar to C4 yet they would identify themselves as a Muslim but with qualification. For example, imagine this dialogue (Muslim questioner in capitals and C5 believer in italics):

ARE YOU A MUSLIM?
What do you mean by Muslim? Was Abraham a Muslim?
YES, OF COURSE.
Did Abraham read the Qur'an?
OF COURSE NOT! IT HAD NOT YET DESCENDED.
Did Abraham know Mohammed?
MOHAMMED (ALAYHI SAHA WA SALAAM) WAS NOT YET BORN.
Well, I am that kind of Muslim. I do not read the Qur'an and I do not know much about Mohammed, but even as Abraham had relationship with God through faith, so do I have relationship with God through faith in Jesus Christ. So yes, I am a Muslim who follows Jesus.

These C5 believers are perceived as a strange type of Muslim.

C6: These are secret believers and are perceived as Muslims. They might or might not be regularly praying at the mosque, but are usually fully integrated into other orthodox community practices.

It should be noted that churches tend to journey up and down the spectrum.

If we take the first Christian believers as examples, they started as C6 (afraid, denying connection to Christ, secret believers). They transitioned to C5, meeting in homes and in the Temple as Jews. Ultimately, as they attained critical mass, they were expelled from mainstream Judaism and met solely in homes as Christians (C4). As the Church became institutionalized over the next 1600 years, it became C3, C2 and even C1 (using Latin in non-Latin speaking contexts).

With the modern missions movement, Moravians (Zinzindorf), coastal missions (Carey), inland missions (Taylor), tribal missions (Townsend/Elliot), unreached peoples (Zwemer) etc., the Church has now begun to move back down the spectrum in contextual (culturally relevant in language, form and structure) ministry. In the Muslim world, most missiologists draw the line at C4 (for the missionaries). They feel it is disingenuous for missionaries to claim the title "Muslim" even with explanatory disclaimers. Muslim Background Believers, however, are encouraged to do so and to even pursue C5 type meetings and approaches. (One missiologist prominent in the OM leadership says that according to his research, most MBBs settle at C4 after missionaries leave.)

	C1	C2	C3	C4	C5	C6
CHRIST-CENTERED COMMUNITY DESCRIPTION	A church foreign to the Muslim community both in culture and language	Like C1, but speaking the language used by Muslims, though their religious terminology is distinctly non-Muslim	Like C2, but using non – Islamic cultural elements (e.g. dress, music, diet and arts)	Like C3, but with some Biblically acceptable Islamic practices	Like C4 with a "Muslim follower of Jesus" self identity	Secret believers, may or may not be active in the religious life of the community
SELF IDENTITY	"Christian" **1%**	"Christian" **4%**	"Christian" **7%**	"Follower of Isa" **60%**	"Muslim follower of Isa" **100%**	Privately "follower of Isa," or "Muslim Follower of Isa"
MUSLIM PERCEPTION	Christian	Christian	Christian	A kind of Christian	A strange kind of Muslim	Muslim

In the Sudanese context it is interesting to see how many MBBs are being discipled in the various modules. Returning to the C1-C6 spectrum, allow me to graph the percentages of these congregations that are MBBs, again in the Sudanese context. (Percentages are superimposed in bold.)

(Percentages can be a little misleading, as seven percent of C3 equals 10 people while 60 percent of C4 equals four people. As C4 groups multiply, the totals will soon outstrip those in C1-C3 models.)

It is self evident that Islam is a collage. There are drastically different attitudes within Islam about Islam itself.

The M1-M9 Spectrum
Muslim Attitudes About Islam (Joshua Massey)

M1	M2	M3	M4	M5	M6	M7	M8	M9
	Muslims Disillusioned With Islam			Muslims Ambivalent About Islam			Muslims Content With Islam	
	Liberal Iranians			Kazakhs			Arabs, South Asians, Indonesians	
High Low Disillusionment			High Low Ambivalence				Low High Contentment	

M1, M2 and M3 Muslims are similar to my friend Mohammed. He hates anything that reminds him of Islam. He does not like Islamic dress, speech or behavior. He loves to read the Bible in English, wear blue jeans and sing along with Hillsong. He is an engineer, bright, articulate and modern. He is as happy as a bug in our C1 church.

M4, M5 and M6 Muslims are pluralistic. They espouse the "I am OK, you are OK" philosophy. They do not fast religiously during Ramadan, nor do they pray five times a day, but they will go to the mosque on Friday and for special occasions. They resent other Muslims who try to convert them and embrace Christians as long as Christians do not try to convert their children. They would happily smile and tell you, "I am a bad Muslim."

M7, M8 and M9 are the missionary Muslims. Not only is Islam the answer for them, it is the answer for the world and they are dedicating to bringing Islam to everyone. Note that though Muslims vary, the majority is M7 to M9.

Because Muslims are so different, they get saved in different ways (as noted by the red arrows in the graph below). This final graph shows the interaction between different types of Muslims and the communities of Christ in which they are being reached and discipled. Religious Muslims (M7, M8, M9) will never set foot in a traditional church, and case studies around the world indicate that they are largely being saved through contextual approaches and being discipled in contextual Christ-like communities.

M1, M2 and M3 Muslims are not attracted by a C4 or C5 approach and often are offended by it. They are primarily being saved in C1, C2 and C3 model communities. Note that around the world M4, M5 and M6-type Muslims are not getting saved anywhere. They have no desire to change, and no Muslim in their right mind will change religion on a whim. Bad Muslims make bad Christians. Pluralistic Muslims have no need to convert.

	C1	C2	C3	C4	C5	C6
CHRIST-CENTERED COMMUNITY DESCRIPTION	A church foreign to the Muslim community both in culture and language	Like C1, but speaking the language used by Muslims, though their religious terminology is distinctly non-Muslim	Like C2, but using non – Islamic cultural elements (e.g. dress, music, diet and arts)	Like C3, but with some Biblically acceptable Islamic practices	Like C4 with a "Muslim follower of Jesus" self identity	Secret believers, may or may not be active in the religious life of the community
SELF IDENTITY	"Christian"	"Christian"	"Christian"	"Follower of Isa"	"Muslim follower of Isa"	Privately "follower of Isa," or "Muslim Follower of Isa"
MUSLIM PERCEPTION	Christian	Christian	Christian	A kind of Christian	A strange kind of Muslim	Muslim

M1	M2	M3	M4	M5	M6	M7	M8	M9
	Muslims Disillusioned With Islam			Muslims Ambivalent About Islam			Muslims Content With Islam	
	Liberal Iranians			Kazakhs			Arabs, South Asians, Indonesians	
High	Low Disillusionment		High	Low Ambivalence		Low	High Contentment	

APPLICATIONS FOR THE SUDANESE CONTEXT

1. Both traditional and contextual models are needed.

    In Sudan, Muslims have definitely been saved in both models.
    More pertinent to this paper, many Muslims who were saved in
    one of the models would never have been saved in the other.

2. In order to be most effective, and because methodologies
    vary so drastically, missionaries/churches should concentrate
    on one model.

    While we agree with Paul in his effort to be "all things to all
    men," we cannot be all things to all men at the same time.
    You cannot reach M1 Muslims and M9 Muslims simultane-
    ously. Paul could not stand on Mars Hill and in the Jerusalem
    Temple in the same instant (nor in the same garb or in the
    same tongue). We need specific approaches for the spe-
    cific Muslim groups. The most effective missionary among
    Muslims is one who is consistent in his approach, while flex-
    ible enough to switch gears if necessary in unique situations
    outside his sphere of influence.

3. There is a need for convergence on a few key issues.

    To this point (February 2004), the traditional Sudanese
    churches largely distrust the contextual model, while a few
    members and ministers within those same churches are
    beginning to experience fruitfulness in contextual outreach.
        In our Port Sudan project, the Sudan Pentecostal Church
    has blessed and commissioned one of its Bible school gradu-
    ates to work with me as a tent-making missionary. As a
    church they will follow a traditional model and even desire
    to buy property and erect a church building in the same city
    one day, but have allowed this man to participate in a totally
    different approach.

In the training initiative (II), some traditional pastors have approved their members to undergo training in planting culturally relevant churches among Muslims and work towards a house church (C4) level movement among Muslims in Sudan.

4. The limited success of the traditional model should not be wielded as a club against the contextual model and vice versa.

The fiercest resistance we have encountered in Sudan against a contextual model has come from Christians (both missionary and national). They have repeatedly argued, "We have MBBs in our church. Why do we have to compromise the gospel to trick others? What we are doing works."

Yes, it does work for some (M1 – M3) but it is failing others. As the above graphs indicate, the majority of Muslims are M7 – M9. They are not being reached in C1 – C3 churches. Therefore, we have a kingdom responsibility to continue in one army with complementing battalions (Similar to Galatians 2, Paul's argument that the gospel for the Jews was committed to Peter as the gospel of the Gentiles was committed to Paul. There is only one gospel but there are different ways to present it.)

MB (an Arab believer who works full-time in reaching Muslims) states that his church (C3) has probably seen 200 Muslims get saved in the last 10 years and only five remain. The primary reason for the attrition? "Our model is not conducive to retaining Muslims. We need a more contextual approach."

CONCLUSION

In Sudan we are on the threshold of great breakthrough among Muslims. The answer is "life on life." We need more missionaries focusing on reaching Muslims. We need more Christian Sudanese focusing on reaching Muslims. We need more traditional churches (C1 – C3) reaching Muslims, and we need more contextual churches (C4 – C5) reaching Muslims. This is Sudan's finest hour and we need unity in our diversity even as the statistical reality reminds us that we have many C1 – C3 models and very few C4 – C5.

Part Three

FIVE MAIN QUESTIONS MUSLIMS ASK CHRISTIANS

Kind, simple and clear responses to the five main questions
that Muslims ask Christians

You cannot live in Sudan without interacting with Muslims. You cannot speak with Muslims as friends, neighbors, employers, employees or colleagues without issues of faith arising. Issues of faith cannot be discussed for long before Muslims raise objections to basic Christian beliefs. Living among Muslims opens a tremendous opportunity for Christian witness. Muslims are by belief and practice very religious. This is to be welcomed not feared. It gives us repeated opportunities to witness. We will look at five main objections Muslims have to Christianity and suggest answers we can respectfully share with them.

> *"In your hearts set apart Christ as Lord. Always be prepared to give an answer to everyone who asks you the reason for the hope that you have. But do this with gentleness and respect, keeping a clear conscience, so that those who speak maliciously against your good behavior in Christ may be ashamed of their slander"* (1 Peter 3:15-16).

Objection 1: The Christian Scripture (Bible) has been corrupted.

When you love Muslims you soon see how much we have in common with them. Christians and Muslims both believe in one God. We believe there are angels and demons. We believe that God has spoken through his prophets. We believe God has left us a reliable written scripture. We believe in the Day of Judgment. We believe that there is an anti-Christ. We believe that there is a Christ and that he will come again. The list goes on.

After some initial agreement and mutual affirmation, we very quickly realize that there are also crucial differences. Christians believe that God is merciful and that sin cannot be forgiven without shed blood (atonement being made). Muslims also believe that God is merciful *but he can forgive our sin without needing to shed anyone's blood.* When it comes to the respective Scripture texts, we run into an impasse:

The Bible records Jesus saying, "I am the way and the truth and the life. No one comes to the Father except through me" (John 14:6).

194

Islam rejects the concept of God as Father. God is not allowed "his one and only Son" (John 3:16; Sura 2:116, 10:68, 19:35, 23:91). The Koran further states: "If any one desires a religion other than Islam, never will it be accepted of him and he will be counted in the ranks of those who are lost" (Sura 3:85).

For servants of the texts of either faith, pluralism is not a viable option. They cannot both be true. If one is right, the other is wrong. Christianity and Islam are mutually exclusive. I often quote the above verses in conversation with Muslim friends. Then with a smile, I slap their knee and say, "My friend, one of us is in serious trouble!"

Most Muslims answer the contradictory issues in Islam and Christianity by saying that the Bible is not trustworthy because it has been corrupted. When a Muslim who doubts the trustworthy nature of the Bible addresses me with such, I respond by respectfully sharing one or more of the following thoughts:

1. Inspiration verses Dictation

I point out that Muslims and Christians have different understandings of how our respective scriptures were revealed. Muslims believe in dictation. God spoke. Gabriel listened and then spoke the exact same words to Mohammed. Mohammed listened and then spoke the exact same words to his followers. The followers listened and then recorded the exact same words on bones, skin and parchment. These recitations were then later compiled into what became known as the Koran.

This means the exact words that God wanted known were passed from God to Gabriel to Mohammed to Muslims. It was an oral dictation that was eventually written and collected. Since the exact words themselves are God-sourced (in Muslim belief), if there is a factual error or grammatical mistake, the backward-traced implication is that God is at fault. A God who makes mistakes? If you point out an error in the Koran, you have succeeded in pointing out an error in God. An errant Koran thus would show that God is not the author of Islam because God cannot make mistakes.

It is this understanding of "dictation, not inspiration" that Muslims apply to our Christian Bible. They do not understand the Christian concept of revelation by inspiration. They view the Bible as if it had been dictated word by word. Scribal notes and errors of transcription in Bible translation over the centuries thus prove to Muslims that the Bible has been corrupted.

Take, for example, 1 John 5:7-8. It seems a great verse for defending the Trinity:

> *"For there are three that testify in heaven: the Father, the Word, and the Holy Spirit, and these three are one. And there are three that testify on earth: the Spirit, the water and the blood; and the three are in agreement".*[2]

The problem is that this verse is not found like this in the most reliable and earliest manuscripts. A scribal note made through time seems to have merged into the text around the 16th century. The earliest collection of Greek manuscripts (called the Majority Text) and the NU collection[3] both indicate that the original text was: "For there are three that testify: the Spirit, the water, and the blood; and the three are in agreement."[4] Muslims use additions such as these in our Bible to claim the Bible cannot be trusted.

They also stumble over parallel passages with apparent discrepancies. For example, who moved David to count the warriors of Israel? Was it God as 2 Samuel 24:1 says? Or was it Satan as 1 Chronicles 21:1 says? Their usual thinking about a God-dictated text sees a contradiction. Christian belief in a God-breathed inspired text[5] is able to recognise the awesome greatness of God. God chooses to weave Satan's work into his own, much greater, purpose. It is as if God says, "You have the freedom to do it, Satan, but I always keep the right to determine the results."

Our Bible was revealed to us through inspiration. God had a certain message that he wanted us to understand, so he whispered it into the souls of prophets and apostles. They in their own hand, in their own dialect and with their own grammar wrote out what God wanted us to know. The result is that 40 different contributors were breathed on by the inspiration of the Holy Spirit. Paul the scholar wrote in Greek language that was quite classical. Peter the fisherman wrote in a more colloquial Greek. Both Paul and Peter tell us something of what God wanted to say. Both communiqués are trustworthy. We hold both together, letting one interpret the other and vice versa. God has clearly revealed to us what he intends us to understand. Whether one writer said, "Thou shalt not steal," and another one wrote, "Do not steal," is of no consequence. We perfectly understand that God does not want us to steal. Matthew records Jesus saying, "Do not judge, or you too will be judged" (Matt. 7:1). John records Jesus saying, "Stop judging by mere appearances, and make a right judgment" (John 7:24). We understand we are to be discerning on spiritual matters but not condemnatory towards anyone. Only God is the Judge (Rom. 2:16).

The Koran never accuses the Bible of being corrupt. Numerous Muslim theologians of the 7th through 10th centuries accepted the truthfulness of Christian Scripture. The word "corrupted" only appears four times in the Koran[6] and it never applies to the Bible itself. It always refers to meaning. Three times it is directed at the Jews and accuses them of changing the meaning of the text. Once it is aimed at Christians, likewise accusing them of changing the meaning of the text to suit their understanding and belief.

The context of these accusations is found in the city of Medina. When Mohammed was originally expelled from Mecca, he travelled to Medina and tried to reach out to the Jewish tribes who lived there. They mocked him (Mohammed was allegedly illiterate) by telling him twisted Bible stories. He subsequently presented a "revelation from God" that was different from the Bible. Names would be wrong, facts would be out of order and the Jews would laugh at Mohammed behind his back. It was this deceit, together with the practice of hypocritically twisting the scriptures to allow their own sinful living that opened Jews and Christians to Mohammed's "corruption" charge. The meaning of the text had been corrupted. The text itself never was.

2. God's Sovereignty

The second response to the Muslim who accuses the Bible of being corrupted is an appeal to the sovereignty of God. When my friend "Joseph" meets a Muslim who accuses the Bible of being corrupted, he lifts his voice so all can hear and says, "God forgive you for your blasphemy! Is God all powerful yet not able to defend his word?" This answer of course demands that the Muslim give justification for his indirect attack on God's ability to defend his revelation. If the Bible was at one time the recorded truth of omnipotent God, how could weak and limited man possible alter it?

Enlarging on this theme, another friend "Maajid" uses the following analogy:

> "I love my son very much. Because Sudan is so hot, whenever my son returns from school, I prepare a cup of cold water for him. I set it on the table and when he walks in, he immediately refreshes himself and quenches his thirst. Let us imagine that my enemy sneaks into my house and replaces that cool water with a cool colourless poison. Under what conditions would I as a father allow my son to drink that poison? It would have to be one of these three. 1) I did not know my enemy had switched the poison. 2) I was afraid or overpowered by my enemy. 3) I did not love my son enough to warn him. Now God is omniscient, omnipotent and all loving. None of the three above explanations can apply to God. Therefore, if the Bible was poisoned, God would have warned us".[7]

If the Bible was poisoned and the Koran was the trustworthy word of God, surely every page of the Koran would shout out a warning. Rather the Koran says: "If you are in doubt about what we have revealed to you, then ask those who have been reading the Book (the Bible) from before you" (Sura 10:94).

3. Chronological Logic

The third response to the Muslim who doubts the trustworthiness of Scripture is to point out the impossibility of his accusation. The Bible could not have been corrupted *before* the Koran was allegedly revealed and collected because the Koran affirms the Bible. If the Bible was corrupted, the Koran is flawed! Yet we have copies of early Bible manuscripts dating to the 3rd and 4th centuries, 100 to 200 *years* before the Koran. The scriptures we have today are the very same scriptures available in Mohammed's day.

Once again the onus of proof is on the disbelieving Muslim. The Bible is innocent until proven guilty. If our Bible is forged, where is the original? If our scripture was corrupted *after* the endorsement given by the Koran, who changed thousands of copies? How is it possible that the translations we use today match those available in 600 AD?

4. Scripture Content
For the sincere Muslim inquirer, for the Muslim who is willing to read the Bible for himself or herself rather than depending on the already biased and twisted thinking of some Islamic apologists, the best appeal we can make is to the Bible itself. If a Muslim can be encouraged to read the Bible with an open heart, over time the word of God changes him or her. Not only will the Bible speak to the heart, it will also speak to the mind. He or she will begin to notice that the God of the Bible is very different from the God of the Koran:

> The Bible will tell the seeker how much God loves him, while the Koran will state five different times that God does not love sinners (Sura 2:190, 2:195, 2:276, 3:31-32, 3:57). The Bible will tell the believer to "love your enemies" (Matthew 5:43-48), while the Koran will tell him to "kill the unbeliever wherever he finds him" (Sura 9:5). The text of the Bible accompanied by the wooing of the Holy Spirit is the best answer to any charge of corruption.

Objection 2: The Trinity is nonsensical.

The central doctrine in Islam is called "tawheed" in Arabic. The word "tawheed" is linked to the noun "waahid," meaning one. In effect it refers to the indivisible oneness of God. God exists in absolute oneness. He will not and he cannot partner with anyone. He is transcendent. No one can partake in God's nature. (Contrast 2 Peter 1:4 which tells us we are partakers of the Divine Nature). According to the Muslim, not only is it impossible for God to be a plurality of oneness, it is abhorrent. The Muslim mind's objection to the Trinity is both empirical and emotional. Christians are accused of making up the doctrine of the Trinity since the word itself is not found in the Bible.

Before I mention some of the more common analogies (all of which break down at some point), let me set the philosophical base for our answer. It is important that we agree with Muslims on a few key points. Our agreement on these does no harm to the truth of the Trinity.

First we agree the Trinity does *not* make sense. If God is transcendent, we as finite humans cannot understand everything he does or he is. If we could completely understand God we would be equal to him. There is an element of trust to all faiths (otherwise they would be called "knows" or "facts," not "faiths"). Muslims and Christians choose at different points to believe what we cannot understand. The word "mu'min" (believer) is applied to both Muslims and Christians in the Koran and in the history of Muslim/Christian dialogue.

Second we agree to underline the omnipotence of God. He is able to do whatever he wills.

Third we agree that the term "Trinity" does not appear in the Bible. But this is not an issue of concern because the term "tawheed" does not exist in the Koran either! Yet "tawheed" has become Islam's cardinal doctrine.

In this discussion with Muslims it is always helpful to point out that there are transferable concepts. This equalizing of the playing field usually does not convince anyone but it lowers the barrier erected by categorical rejection of the other's view. If the Muslim can admit to the necessity of trust in his or her own faith, he cannot deny another.

Now let me illustrate how this can be done when talking to Muslims about the Trinity. In the Koran there is the famous verse that refers to Jesus as "The Word of God and a Spirit from Him" (Sura 4:171). I find it interesting to ask Muslims if Islam teaches a duality in the Godhead. Is God separate from his Word? Which came first? Was his word created? There has to be simultaneity of existence. If God existed from eternity past without his Word, was he mute? What about the Spirit of God? Did God exist without his Spirit? How could that be? When did God's Spirit start? To the Muslim it is obvious that from eternity past God had a voice (his Word) and God was alive (his spirit). In a way the Trinity of God/Word/Spirit is already at hand for the Muslim.

This is of course the best analogy to use. The Biblical view of Jesus as the Word of God, the Holy Spirit as the Spirit of God and the Fatherhood of God is not so far a leap from the Islamic understanding of God, God's Word and God's Spirit. The obvious gap is the Fatherhood of God, which Islam rejects categorically. It is wise to begin any explanation by making sure that Muslims know we do *not* believe the old Marianite heresy of a God/Mary/Jesus Trinity. It was this false teaching that fostered a misunderstanding in 5th century Arabia and prompted some of the Koran's verses against supposedly Christian teaching.

Fallible Analogies

Let me repeat the disclaimer that while analogies can help, they all break down at some point. Here are some of the common ones that can be used. I will list them in order of my personal preference:

- *God/Word/Spirit (detailed above)*
- *One Human as Father/Brother/Son*
  In conversation with Muslims I will often use the people themselves as examples:

  "Is your father living? I am sure you are a faithful son to your father. Have you any brothers? How many? I am sure you are a good brother to your brothers. How many children do you have? I can see that you are a loving father to your children. My friend, do you see the point I am making? You are a father, a brother and a son but you are one person. You respond in different ways to these varied groups of people, but you remain absolutely one individual."

The main shortcoming of this analogy is that unlike any human being God is eternally all that he is. There never was a time when he was not all that he is.

• *Mind/Thought/Analysis*

My mind (not my brain) is an abstract. With my faculty of thinking I can dwell on one thought. As I dwell on that thought, I can analyse whether that thought is noble, selfish or trivial. Thus I have a plurality in thought of thinking ability, thought and analysis of thought. The main shortcoming of this analogy is that God is not influenced or controlled by anything outside of himself. He is always God in and of himself.

• *Fire/Light/Heat*

One fire gives off light and heat as it burns. The Bible says, "God is a consuming Fire" (Hebrews 12:29). The main shortcoming of this analogy is that God needs nothing outside of himself in order to exist. A fire needs wood or charcoal and must be lit by someone or something. God is fully self-existent.

• *Body/Soul/Personality*

One person is made of a physical body plus their psyche (mind and spirit). Every one of us behaves individually and uniquely in a way others recognise as being "us." Again the main shortcoming of this analogy is that God has no beginning and no end, unlike every human being. Nor are there three parts adding up to one God as a mathematical sum: $1+1+1=3$. God forever has been and will be Father, Son and Holy Spirit.

The Holy Trinity may be "nonsensical" but it is not foolish nonsense. Inspired thinking of God in this way enlarges our wonder and admiration for his greatness, his "otherness." Our human minds and our hearts bow in worship before him.

Objection 3: The Atonement is not necessary.

Muslims do not believe in original sin. While they believe that every person (with the exception of Jesus, Mary and John the Baptist, according to tradition) was touched with sin at birth, they do not believe that sin is inherent to the human race, carried in our spiritual DNA.

Further they believe that God is merciful and if God wants to forgive sin, he certainly can. He does not need to vengefully kill someone else in order for his mercy to be shown. If God wants to forgive, he will forgive. We can sway his opinion of course by a life of good works and veneration of the prophet Mohammed (who can put in a good word for you on Judgment Day if you have honoured him well). The result is a works-oriented religion with a lack of eternal assurance. At the end of the day if you have more merit than sin, you will end up in heaven. Even this balance is tempered by the fact that God alone decides. No one can know personal salvation for sure.

In dialogue with Muslims, I have found two hypothetical situations of great help in explaining the Christian view. The first deals with the faulty logic behind *any* works-oriented tradition and the second with the need for atonement, not just forgiveness.

1. Practising Muslims do not eat pork. I will ask them this series of questions:

    Question: "If you went to the butcher, would you buy minced meat from him if you knew that the meat was 90 percent pork and only 10 percent beef?"
    Answer: "Of course not!"

    Question: "What if you knew the minced meat was 90 percent beef

and only 10 percent pork?"
Answer: "Of course not!"

Question: "What if the minced meat was 99 percent beef and only 1 percent pork?"
Answer: "I will never touch anything that has been defiled by pork, not even if it is one tiny drop."

Question: "Then how can you hold Holy God to a higher standard than your own? How could a Holy God possibly allow a person with even 1 percent of sin into his presence?"

2.   **A family and a judge.** I ask the Muslim how he would feel about a judge who pardoned a thief, murderer and rapist:

"Let us pretend," I say, "that a thief enters your house and steals all your money. The thief is caught and brought before the judge. The judge tells the thief, 'What you have done is sinful but because I am merciful, I forgive and release you.' The thief thanks the judge and that night returns to your house and kills all your children. Again the thief is caught and brought before the judge. "What you have done is very sinful, but I am very merciful, so I forgive you and free you again." The thief thanks the judge and returns to your house that night and rapes your wife. Again he is caught and again the merciful judge forgives and frees him. What would you think of that judge? Would you respect him? He is merciful but he is not just. Atonement brings together both the justice and the mercy of God."

A further objection that Muslims have regarding the atoning death of Christ is the element of suffering. Muslims cannot believe that God would allow one of his Prophets to experience a shameful defeat or death. Muslims deny that Jesus was literally crucified and claim that either Judas was put up on the cross by mistake or Jesus "swooned" on the cross; he did not actually die.

These denials of Jesus' death seem to run counter to the Koran itself. In Koran 3:55, God is speaking and says, "I will cause

(Jesus) to die...." In 5:117, Jesus refers to "...when you caused me to die...." In 19:33, Jesus again says, "Peace upon me the day that I was born and the day that I die." All three references use the Arabic verb "itwaffa," the same verb that is used today for "death." Koran 4:157 does say, "You did not kill him, you did not crucify him" but the text shows that this comment was directed at the Jews and is in line with the claim of Jesus as recorded in the Gospel, "No one takes my life from me, but I lay it down of my own accord" (John 10:17-18).

When presenting the Biblical view of atonement, the logical starting place is the absolute holiness of God. We humans are in an impossible situation. God is so holy that he only allows 100 percent perfect people into his presence, and yet no one is nor can be 100 percent holy. No one can attain the level of holiness that God demands.

With this foundation, we need to show that God, from the very first sin, shed blood to cover the sin. Adam and Eve tried to clothe themselves with leaves (Gen. 3:7) but God killed an animal and covered their sin with skin from the animal that he shed its blood (3:21). The Old Testament story reveals progressively how every sin had to be covered by blood. Abraham on Mt. Moriah tells his son that "God will provide a lamb" (22:8). In the New Testament John the Baptist points to Jesus and says, "Look, the Lamb of God, who takes away the sin of the world" (John 1:29)! In the whole Bible context, we see God has always insisted: "Without the shedding of blood there is no forgiveness" (Heb. 9:22).

Most Muslims are from cultures that appreciate indirection and stories. I have found the best way to illustrate vicarious atonement is by using the following story:

> "In San Francisco at the turn of the 20th century, there lived two immigrant Chinese brothers. The elder brother was industrious and moral. He feared God and lived in right relationship with his community. The younger brother was mischievous, rebellious and violent. He loved to frequent the bars and brothels. The older brother repeatedly warned and pleaded with his younger brother whom he

loved to turn from his sinful ways and live a godly life. The younger man happily ignored all his brother's pleas.

One fateful night the younger brother got into a brawl at the local bar. Smashing a beer bottle on a nearby table, he used the sharp end as a club with which to kill a man. Blood from his victim's clothes splattered all over his shirt. The police were called and the younger brother ran home in abject fear. His older brother welcomed him in and on hearing his frantic confession calmly told him to take off his shirt. The innocent brother exchanged the guilty brother's shirt for his own. The police arrived and not able to distinguish one immigrant Chinese from another hustled the innocent elder brother in the bloodstained shirt to prison. In the course of time, this righteous brother was tried, sentenced and executed.

Five years passed and as time went by, the guilty feelings of the younger brother increased. He came to a point where he could bear no more. He sought out the judge who had sentenced his older brother to death. He confessed through his tears, "I am the guilty one. My precious brother was innocent of any wrong. He died in my place. What can be done?" The judge was quiet for a moment. Then he gently said, "Blood has been shed. The debt has been paid. You are free to go."

Objection 4: Jesus is not God.

Every Muslim is quick to affirm that Muslims believe in Jesus. Most will admit him into the top three Prophets of importance alongside Moses and Mohammed. They will agree that Jesus was a prophet, a teacher and a miracle worker. But the concept of Jesus as God is blasphemous to a Muslim.

The Koran gives us a great starting point on this question. In numerous places the Koran affirms the uniqueness of Jesus (19:18-19, 3:45, 4:171). He is called the Messiah, the Word of God, Virgin Born and recognised as coming again to judge the living and the dead. The Hadiith even affirms that Jesus is sinless.[8] I love to start any discussion on the nature of Jesus by summarising what Islam admits about him: Messiah, sinless, the Word of

God, born of a virgin and returning Judge. I then bridge to the story of Jesus healing the paralytic man and forgiving his sins (Mark 2:1-12). I mention all the things that Jesus has done for me (loved, forgiven, healed, blessed, comforted, forgiven sin and granted heaven) and I ask what anyone else can possibly do. Jesus is very special!

Proving the deity of Jesus outside of the authority of scripture is another matter. We sometimes demand belief prematurely. We need to allow Muslims time to come and trust the Scripture, listening to the advice of the Holy Spirit. Jesus' first disciples journeyed progressively into their understanding of the nature of Christ. Several centuries and councils of our church fathers were needed to clarify our own understandings. We must introduce Muslims to Jesus. When they fall in love with him (and most of them do before they understand that he is God), there starts a relational base of trust on which the Holy Spirit can secure the heavy truth of Jesus' divinity.

We should never refer to the Koran in any way that gives it authority. All of our references should be in question form: Why does the Koran say this or that? When we ask Muslims questions about the Koran, we do not affirm it as authoritative. We invite them to begin to question it. We should never use the Koran to try and prove the Bible or any Christian doctrine as true. Why? If you do so, the progression is simple and dangerous:

1) You use the Koran to prove the Bible is true.
2) The Bible reveals that the Koran is false.
3) If the Koran is false, how can you use it to verify the Bible?
4) What it says about the Bible must also be false.

It is neither advisable nor fair to compare Jesus to Mohammed. Jesus never sinned and Mohammed had to repent numerous times (Koran 4:96-97; 40:54-55; 47:19). Comparison is not advisable because we anger Muslims and the red fog of anger then removes any possibility of amicable discussion. Comparison is not fair because Orthodox Islam never claims Mohammed to be perfect nor to be the incarnation of God. The Koran is claimed as absolutely perfect. It is not too much to say, though, that Islam and Christianity are delineated thus:

> In Islam the Word of God became a book (Koran).
> In Christianity the Word of God became a person (Jesus).

Any fair comparisons should compare Jesus to the Koran, the Christian Word of God compared with the Muslim word of God. If you can point to an error in Jesus, Christianity crumbles. If you can point to an error in the Koran, Islam fails. Fallibility in the life of Mohammed is not central to this argument.

The fact that Mohammed gave fallible advice (see the Hadith of Sahiih Muslim "Ridaat al Kabiir" # 1453), sanctioned assassinations, led 29 different violent attacks and took 12 different wives plus numerous concubines (including one who was 6-years-old and another he asked his adopted son to divorce so he could marry) is not the point. If a Muslim wants to compare and contrast Mohammed to Jesus, we will be delighted to do so. No right-thinking Muslim will dare as it is not a favourable comparison for their prophet.

If a Muslim knows the biographical history of Mohammed and presses the point, I usually find it enough to ask this rhetorical question: "If Jesus was at one well and Mohammed was at another, to which well would you send your wife to draw water?"

Objection 5: God cannot have a Son.

Muslims will tell you repeatedly that "God does not begat, nor was he begotten" and "God cannot take the form of his creation." The unpardonable sin in Islam is "shirk" which comes from the verb "sharaka," to associate or partner. To ascribe an equal to God is the most offensive thing one could do because it violates God's "tawheed," his incomparable oneness.

The term "Son of God" therefore makes Muslims recoil. It

is incomprehensible and reprehensible to Muslims to even suggest that God would have physical relations with Mary in order to produce Jesus. Again, the original confusion is linked to the Marianite heresy, which taught a Mary-included Trinity. Modern Roman Catholicism has not helped by its over-exaltation of Mary.

Our response begins with the explanation of metaphor. Remember that Muslims acknowledge the virgin birth. We must simply affirm that Jesus was virgin born and that "Son of" is a metaphor for a unique relationship. In the Koran the expression "son of the road" is used to refer to a traveller (Koran 2:177). Sudanese and Egyptians are often referred to today as "sons of the Nile." In discussion with Muslims I will often ask with a smile, "So tell me: who had sex with the road to produce travellers? And who had sex with the Nile in order to produce you wonderful Sudanese?" The response is always a playful chuckle and the metaphor point is acknowledged.

A second means of explanation is to ask, "Who was the father of Adam? If God is Adam's father, then can we call Adam a son of God? Imagine you were the recording official when Jesus was born. You were in charge of filling out Jesus' birth certificate. Who would you write in the space marked 'Father'?"

One Khartoum summer on a boat steaming up the Nile, I was sitting next to a dear friend who was a recent convert to Christ. He was asking this very question about the incarnation. I had a teacup in my hand and with it I pointed to the Nile.

I asked him, "What water is that?"

"The Nile," he said.

I dipped the cup down into the water and lifted it out again. "And what water is this?"

He smiled and said, "That too is the Nile."

"And what is the difference between this Nile and that Nile?"

"None," he said.

I threw the water from the cup back into the Nile and said. "Jesus is the essence of God. He came to the earth in human form for 33 short years. Then he returned to heaven."

This simple (and imperfect) illustration was enough for my friend. Since that day, the incarnation of Jesus has not been a problem for him. Let me be sure to say the illustration helped largely because my friend *wanted* to understand. God had made him ready. For others who seek to undermine and accentuate problematic issues, this analogy is limited. Again, let me repeat what I mentioned earlier. Cleverness and polemic argument wins very few Muslims to Jesus. There are thousands of Muslims much smarter and more articulate than you or I. Muslims have been deceived and blinded by the devil and unless the Lord intervenes, none of our illustrations or answers will be decisive in the battle for their souls (2 Corinthians 4:4; Acts 16:14).

I used to think that if only I could learn Arabic, acculturate the message and live contextually, then Muslims would instantly embrace the gospel. Unfortunately I found out this is not so. Almost every Muslim I know who now follows Jesus has journeyed through several years of searching and questioning.

There are usually three encounters that work together as Muslims come to know Jesus as Saviour and Lord:

1) Love encounter and ongoing relationship with a Christian.
2) Truth encounter and ongoing study of the Bible.
3) Power encounter (a dream, miracle or supernatural sign).

In the end, and following Christians in all ages, we rely on prayer. Yes, we study hard. Yes, we learn how to gracefully "give an answer to everyone who asks us the reason for the hope that we have" (1 Peter 3:15-16). Yes, we learn Arabic. Yes, we don the robe and drape the veil. Yes, we love and listen to Muslims year after year. We do all this gladly but we know there is no "magic" formula. We have only the assurance that every person's salvation is a miracle. We know that every person's salvation is a very personal encounter between one soul and one Saviour. And we know the only Saviour is Jesus the Messiah (Acts 4:12).

ENDNOTES

1 With the exception of greeting the recording angels at the end of the ritual prayer, examples can be found for standing, bowing, kneeling, prostrating and lifting hands in prayer all throughout the Bible. "Islamic" forms then are effectually adapted from Biblical patterns.

2 See NIV footnote of 1 John 5:7-8.

3 Two translators use the Alexandrian/Egyptian manuscripts in their critical publishing: Nestle-Aland in the 26th edition of the Greek New Testament and United Bible Society 3rd edition. The translators of the New King James Version consulted these sources. New King James Version, (Nashville: TN, Thomas Nelson, Inc., 1982), vi.

4 See NIV text of 1 John 5:7-8.

5 2 Timothy 3:16-17.

6 Koran 2:75-79; 3:71; 4:46; 5:13-14.

7 See Gal. 1:6-9.

8 "Bukhari," University of Southern California, Compendium of Muslim Texts, http://www.usc.edu/dept/MSA/fundamentals/hadithsunnah/bukhari/054. sbt.html (accessed 12 November 2008), Volume 4, Book 54, Number 506.

Printed in the United States
218188BV00002B/2/P